Dimensions in F

Movement and Change

Series Editor: Angela Wood

ANGELA WOOD

JOHN LOGAN

JENNY ROSE

Nelson

Acquisitions: Lisa Thomas, Brenda Eisenberg
Administration: Eileen Regan
Editorial: Catherine Dakin
Marketing: Jeremy Warner
Production: Tony Warner
Staff design: Lorraine Inglis
Design: Nigel Jordan
Illustrations: Clinton Banbury, Nigel Jordan,
Lotty, Allen Wittert
Cover illustration: Cathy Morley

Thomas Nelson and Sons Ltd
Nelson House, Mayfield Road
Walton-on-Thames, Surrey
KT12 5PL, UK

Thomas Nelson Australia
102 Dodds Street
South Melbourne
Victoria 3205, Australia

Nelson Canada
1120 Birchmount Road
Scarborough, Ontario
M1K 5G4, Canada

© Angela Wood, John Logan and Jenny Rose 1997

First published by Thomas Nelson and Sons Ltd 1997

I(T)P® Thomas Nelson is an International Thomson
Publishing Company
I(T)P® is used under licence

ISBN 0-17-437067-9
NPN 9 8 7 6 5 4 3 2 1

Acknowledgements
The publishers are grateful to the following for
permission to reproduce copyright material:

Andes Press Agency p. 60 (bottom); Christian Aid
pp. 44, 45; Chris Fairclough pp. 22 (bottom), 24;
Gamma p. 62 (top left); Guy Hall pp. 4 (top right),
14 (top), 17 (bottom), 22 (top), 38 (bottom right), 42, 43
(bottom), 46, 50 (top and bottom right, bottom centre),
51 (bottom), 58, 59 (bottom), 65, 69, 74, 78 (bottom),
88, 95 (all); Hutchison Library pp. 10, 38 (top two and
bottom left), 74; Image Bank p. 43 (left); Image Select
pp. 6 (top), 29 (top centre, top left and bottom right),
30, 34, 59 (top); Panos Pictures pp. 8, 9 (bottom);
Ann & Bury Peerless p. 17 (top right), 29 (top right, top
centre, centre and bottom centre), 80 (top); Spectrum
Colour Library pp. 6 (bottom), 50 (bottom left);
David Rose pp. 21, 70-71, 78 (top left); Jenny Rose p. 7;
Tony Stone pp. 4 (top left), 50 (top right and centre), 62;
Trip pp. 4 (bottom right), 14 (bottom), 16 (top two), 20,
27, 29 (bottom left), 32, 33, 36 (bottom), 43 (top), 48, 51
(top), 59 (centre), 68, 75, 78 (top left and centre), 79,
86, 89 (both), 91, 92 (both); Angela Wood pp. 4 (bottom
left), 16 (bottom), 36 (top), 41, 72, 79 (bottom left), 84,
93 (top)

Although every effort has been made to trace original
sources and copyright holders, this has not been
possible in all cases. The publishers will be pleased to
rectify any such omission in future editions.

The authors and publishers would like to thank the staff
and pupils of the following schools.

Darton High School, Barnsley; Bristnall Hall High
School, Warley; Fairwater Comprehensive School,
Gwent; Cirencester Deer Park School, Cirencester;
Lings Upper School, Northampton; Heworth Grange
Comprehensive School, Tyne & Wear; St Matthew's RC
Primary School, Glasgow; The Deepings School,
Peterborough; Pimlico School, London; Dromore High
School, County Down

Contents

Throughout this series you will see the following symbols. Each symbol represents a religion or religious tradition. Whenever a particular religion or religious tradition is being discussed, you will see its symbol.

 Buddhism

 Judaism

Christianity

Rastafari

Hinduism

Sikhism

 Islam

1 I Wonder...

This chapter is about:

- the mystery of the world we live in and the ways we express our feelings about that mystery
- how religious traditions express their awareness of the presence of God
- signposts to God: Christian art and architecture
- words as worship: Sikh morning prayers

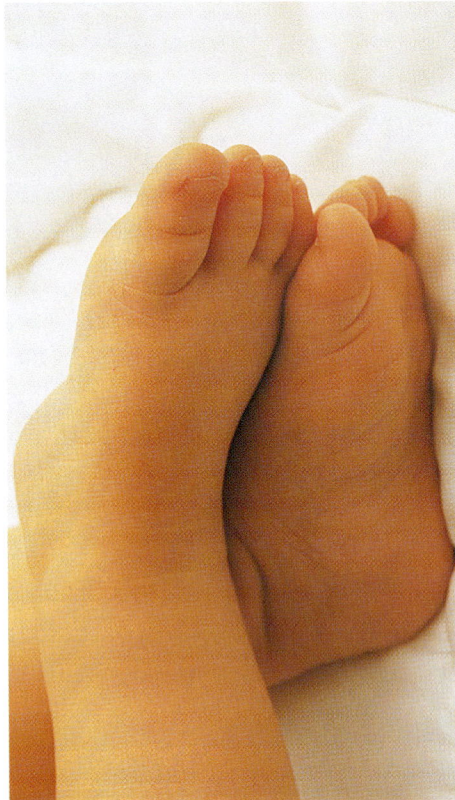

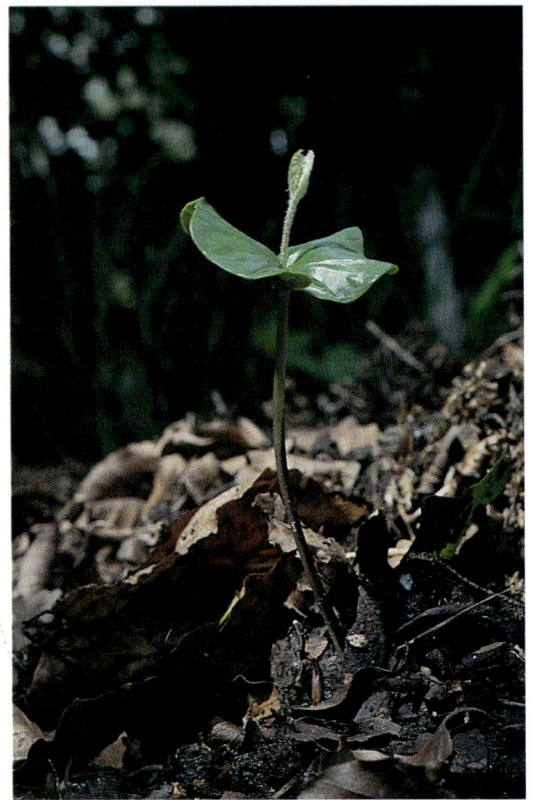

Think of the Maker

Think of a time when you saw that the world is beautiful...
Think of a sunset over the hills, or sunrise over a sleeping city.
Think of a running river, or stars shining on a dark sea.
Think of light flashing on a puddle, or of geraniums growing in
* a window box.*
Think of a time when you saw that the world is beautiful – and
* give thanks...*

From an Iona Community meditation.

A sense of wonder?

The images in the pictures opposite are full of energy, but also have a quality of stillness about them. Images like these often 'move' or 'touch' people very deeply. They might even make them react strongly – just as people at a fireworks display exclaim 'ooh' and 'aah' as each new colour and pattern shoots and sprays over the dark sky. What other images have you seen that you find have power and mystery? Can you think of both natural and humanly-created examples? Are they all beautiful? Or are some disturbing?

*Often our experience of life leads us to ask difficult questions. When we see how complex the universe is, with its rhythm and order, we might wonder what **our** place is in the world. We might ask questions like: 'Why am I here?' or 'What happens when we die?' These are questions about the meaning and purpose of our life. People have asked questions like these for a long time yet there are no single, straight answers that could ever be the same for everyone. What are **your** 'big questions about life'?*

The religions of the world answer the 'big questions about life' in many different ways but in all religions people feel there is a creative energy or a sacred dimension in life. They usually say that they cannot understand it or put it into words, and they respond to it in a different way – their own way. Each religious tradition has its own teaching about that creative energy or sacred dimension in life. They may create beautiful architecture, works of art and literature. They may develop rituals, prayers and forms of meditation: all of these are ways that people explore and express the sense of something holy.

Signposts to God: Christian art and architecture

Art is one of the ways that people express their sense that God is present in the world and imitate or reflect God's creativity. Christians in the Middle Ages often thought of God as the 'Great Architect of Creation' and many manuscripts of the time show God holding compasses or dividers. Building places of worship gave Christians the feeling that they were carrying on God's work in the world and coming closer to him.

Many medieval cathedrals have a rose window. As a beautiful combination of shape, colours and images, the rose window symbolises the wholeness of Creation, and the endless power of God.

The Nave, York Minster.

For centuries, Christians have built grand, beautiful churches to glorify God. In the past, designing, building and decorating a church was as much an act of worship as coming to pray inside the church. The work of building great cathedrals, in particular, showed great devotion, patience and creativity. The early cathedral builders believed their work was in some way in touch with the infinite, eternal glory of God, acting like a signpost to heaven. Still today, some Christians see their places of worship – churches, chapels and meeting-houses, as well as cathedrals – as 'sanctuaries in space', places where God can be found and felt.

Abbot Suger was responsible for rebuilding a French abbey in the early 12th century. He thought that through the splendour and beauty of Christian art and architecture, people could have an experience of the presence and power of God. Many church architects since then have also designed places of worship that they hope will give a glimpse of the wonder of God.

The church

This passage describes how a young boy, who has spent all his life imprisoned in a camp and has now escaped to Italy, ventures inside a church for the first time. He has a clear idea of what God means to him and calls God the 'God of the green pastures and still waters'. He is not sure of anyone else's God, however. As you read the description, try to picture the building in your mind. Are there any parts of David's impressions and experiences of the church that you can relate to?

David stood in the open space that was always to be found in front of a church and wondered if he dared. He had wanted for such a long time to see what a church was like. A church was a place where you talked with God. In Italy, of course, he would only find the God of the Roman Catholics, but still – suppose his own God were on a visit there! And suppose he really met Him! But perhaps Gods did not visit one another... However, a faint hope that he would find some comfort there drove him inside.

The door was very heavy. He had to push hard to open it. The light inside was very subdued. David remained standing just inside the door until his eyes had grown accustomed to the change from the bright sunlight outside to the soft obscurity within.

It was very quiet. And beautiful. It reminded him a little of a house, though in many ways it was very different. There were paintings and carved woodwork and coloured glass in the windows. In front of some of the paintings along the side of the church, candles were burning.

From Anne Holm, *I Am David*, Methuen, 1965

Modern churches are built with different materials and in a different way from older cathedrals but they still have a sense of 'otherness' or 'holiness' about them. This church in Helsinki, Finland, is built out of solid rock, but has a glass roof so that people inside can feel there is nothing between them and the sky.

Images of Christ

For all Christians, Jesus Christ is the focus of worship, or the path to it. For them, one of the most wonderful acts of God in history was when he was born as a human being, Jesus Christ. John's Gospel describes this as: 'the Word became flesh and dwelt among us, full of grace and truth' (John 1:14). Most Christians believe that Jesus was both fully human and fully divine and that he opened the way to the kingdom of God. Paul said that the glory of God is reflected in the face of Jesus Christ (2 Corinthians 4: 6).

Even though Jesus may be one of the most famous people who ever lived, no one now knows what he looked like. The Gospels, which were written decades after he died, do not describe his physical appearance. Other writings of that time give only a brief, vague description and may not be reliable. Most Christians would probably say that what Jesus looked like doesn't matter at all: it is who and what he was and is that counts. This means that no one can ever say that a painting of him is 'wrong'. Every artist will depict Jesus in the way that he or she 'sees' him. Most artists portray Jesus as a member of the society in which they live, looking and behaving much like the people around them.

Each artist has to decide whether to emphasise Jesus Christ's humanity or divinity. As a human, Jesus can identify with the needs and feelings of other humans; as divine he can overcome the evil and suffering of the world. Many pictures combine both elements and put across a powerful message about the person of Jesus that points the viewer beyond the picture.

This is a mural in Changar, in the Tete province of Mozambique. It shows Jesus' mother, Mary, approaching him as he addresses crowds of people. Both of them have haloes. The artists have painted the scene as though it was taking place near their village rather than in the land of Israel of the 1st century.

'Yellow Christ' by the French artist Paul Gaugin. This image is very different from traditional images. But, like Christian artists everywhere, Gaugin shows Jesus in his, the artist's, own time and place. The striking colour that Gaugin uses for Jesus' skin contrasts with the skin tones of the peasants and with the landscape of the countryside, making Jesus 'stand out' or 'in another world'.

As well as paintings and sculptures, one way of portraying the life of Jesus is through acting out important events in his life. This is a scene on Good Friday during Semana Santa (Holy Week) in Antigua, Guatemala. The man on the roof is taking the part of Jesus, carrying his cross on the way to his death. The people below are taking the parts of Jews of the 1st century in the land of Israel and also Roman soldiers who were occupying the land. 'Jesus' is high up to show his importance and so that everyone can see him. For many Christians in Central and South America, Jesus is real because he shares their experiences and lives amongst them as one of the poor and the oppressed.

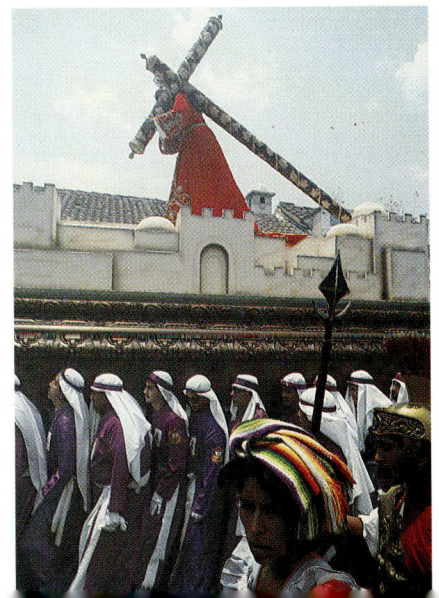

Words as worship: Sikh morning prayers

Sikhs believe that people are in an endless cycle of life, death and rebirth: they are born time and time again until they can escape from this world. Birth is a great opportunity to attain that release or liberation. Sikhs believe that everyone can reach liberation in this life through becoming God-conscious and God-filled, aware of God as an inner presence.

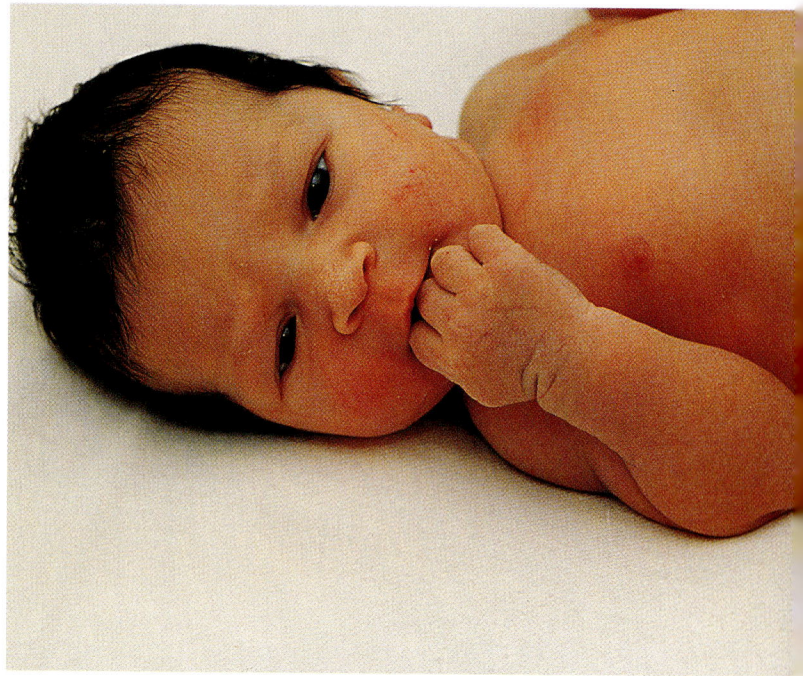

The Mul Mantra

There is but one God;
Eternal Truth is his name.
Creator of all things,
Fearless and without hatred,
Timeless and formless,
Beyond birth and death,
Self-existent,
Known through his grace.

Sikhs worship the one 'formless' God, who is present, not just in each human being, but in every part of the universe. Guru Nanak, the first of the Sikh teachers, sang of the wonders of the mountains, rivers, woods and plants which were witness to the creative work of God. The Sikh tradition emphasises the oneness of God and the oneness of humanity. The **Mul Mantra**, the text by Guru Nanak that appears at the beginning of the Guru Granth Sahib, sums up the Sikh belief in God.

In their time, the Sikh Gurus (the founders of Sikhism) constantly emphasised the need for each person's mind to be focused on God, so that everything they did would be in praise of God. Although meditation is important, there is no tradition of concentrating on an image, a picture of a person, or a piece of art. Instead, Sikhs focus on God, who is often referred to as **Sat Nam** – the True Name, or **Waheguru** – Wonderful Lord. For them, meditation is not a mechanical repetition of a phrase or a religious text, but involves thinking about and concentrating on God's nature. Some devout Sikhs meditate in the morning before saying the prescribed prayers. They wrap themselves in a woollen or cotton shawl, close their eyes and recite *'Waheguru, Waheguru'* for as long as they can.

For Sikhs, the words of the Guru Granth Sahib are living expressions of the presence and purpose of God. The scriptures are the place where God is to be found in all his power and glory.

> *The Word is a shower of Nectar,*
> *By the grace of Guru, it rains eternally on my mind.*
> *Being coloured with the hue of the Creator,*
> *The Word leads one to the vision of the Lord.*
>
> Adi Granth

Morning prayer

Each morning, Sikhs get up early, take a bath or shower, and recite the Mul Mantra, then the Japji Sahib prayer in their homes. These prayers were composed by Guru Nanak 500 years ago and are found at the beginning of the Guru Granth Sahib.

Many Sikhs know the Japji Sahib by heart and recite it while getting ready for the day, before breakfast. For some, it is a meditation in itself while doing household chores. Some read the prayer from the Sikh prayer book called **Gutka**, while others may listen to it on cassette.

> *The Japji Sahib*
>
> *God is not to be comprehended by human thought,*
> *Though we may try it a hundred thousand times.*
> *Outward silence cannot still the mind's search for truth,*
> *Though we absorb ourselves in meditation long and deep.*
> *Our hunger for God can never be satisfied,*
> *Even if we acquire everything the universe has to offer.*
> *If we increase our wisdom beyond measure,*
> *It is still not enough.*
> *How, then, can we come to know the truth?*
> *How can the veil of falsehood be torn asunder?*
> *By following God's will, O Nanak,*
> *Which is written within our hearts.*
>
> First stanza, translated by Piara Singh Sambhi

Native Americans traditionally live close to nature and find its beauty wonderful and awesome, as in this poem by a Native American Chief.

And My Heart Soars

The beauty of the trees,
the softness of the air,
the fragrance of the grass,
*   speak to me.*

The summit of the mountain,
the thunder of the sky,
the rhythm of the sea,
*   speak to me.*

The faintness of the stars,
the freshness of the morning,
the dewdrop on the flower,
*   speak to me.*

The strength of fire,
the taste of salmon,
the trail of the sun,
*   – and the life that never goes away,*
*   speak to me.*

And my heart soars.

Chief Dan George, Hancock House Publishing Ltd

Questions and activities

1 Read the poems 'Think of the Maker' on page 5 and 'And My Heart Soars' on page 12. Also, look at the pictures on page 4.

   A What have you thought, felt or sensed that has 'made your heart soar'?

   B Group these thoughts, feelings and sensations under the headings **Natural World** (e.g. falling leaves, the sound of birds, waves in the sea) and **Humanly Created World** (e.g. a piece of music, Concorde in flight, computers).

   C Make a collage of all these images, using your own drawings or cut-out pictures, or a combination of both.

2 Read page 5.

   A What three 'big questions about life' would you want to ask the wisest person in the world?

   B Share your questions with a partner and act as the 'wisest person in the world' for each other, answering the questions in the form of a story or picture if possible.

3 On page 7, read the extract from *I am David* about David's first experience of a church.

   A Picture the building in your mind. Write down words to describe the building that come into your head.

   B Look at the pictures of churches on pages 6–7. Describe each one, as if you were standing outside and then entering the church for the first time.

4 Look at the different images of Christ on pages 8–9.

   A Describe his features in each one.

   B What kind of person or being is Jesus shown as, in each one?

5 Read the section on the Sikh morning prayer on pages 10–11. Summarise Sikh beliefs about:

   ● God as Creator

   ● consciousness of God

   ● the Guru Granth Sahib

2 Beyond Words

This chapter is about:
- the many forms of worship
- meditation
- Charismatic Christian worship
- words and sounds in Rastafari life and worship

Many kinds of 'special'

On their wedding anniversary, Don and Ginny were going to have a meal together at home and then go out. Don gave Ginny a pair of slippers and Ginny gave Don a sweater. Ginny loved her new slippers, tried them on – and wrapped them up in the tissue and put the box in the wardrobe. Then she went into the kitchen to cook, wearing her old slippers. Don loved his new sweater, tried it on – and then went outside to get the car going properly. When he came in to eat, Ginny was upset because there was grease on his sweater. But Don was also upset with Ginny… ■

Why do you think Don and Ginny were upset with each other? How were they different in the ways they showed their presents were 'special'?

Many people think worship is like the way Ginny treated her present: it's so special that you must keep it carefully and, in a way, 'away' from life. But worship is also like the way Don treated his present: it's so special that you must have it with you all the time, right in the middle of life. You can see these two approaches (or combinations of them) in the many ways that religious traditions have developed worship – sometimes even within the same tradition.

Some people say that their whole life is worship: they do not mean that they pray all day but that whatever they do is a way of offering their life, of reaching out to something greater than them. And that the ultimate being that they may call 'God' reaches out to them in many ways, as well. This modern Jewish parable is about the need to see and respond to God in the midst of life:

The floods were unexpected and it was all systems go to save the community before the waters engulfed the valley. One family was trapped in their home and neighbours urged them to escape with them in their cart. 'We have trust in God,' the father called from the window. 'Don't be afraid. He'll save you, too. We're not moving.'

The waters rose quickly and they were forced upstairs. A passing boatman beckoned to them. 'Our faith will not waver,' replied the mother. 'Peace be with you.'

Finally, on the roof of their home, refusing to catch hold of a lowered rope ladder, they waved the helicopter off and the children chorused, 'We have believed in God all our lives. God will not let us down.'

Shoulder to shoulder, they faced the Almighty, with heavy hearts and harsh voices. 'How could you! We have been your faithful servants – surely we deserved better! Why didn't you help us?'

'But I did,' said God. 'I sent you the neighbours with the cart. I sent you the boat. I sent you the helicopter.'

Angela Wood and Robin Richardson, *Inside Stories: Wisdom and Hope for Changing Worlds*, Trentham Books, 1992

The world of worship

Buddhist prayer flags, Bhutan. As these 'flags' flutter in the breeze, the expressions of loving kindess written on them are sent out into the world.

An Orthodox Christian kissing an ikon as an expression of devotion, respect and love.

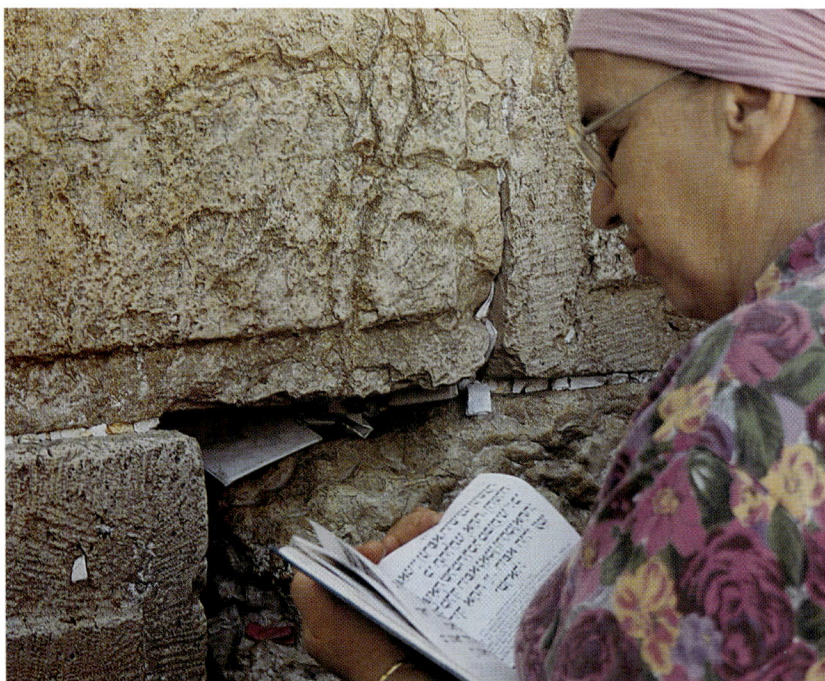

The Western Wall – the only remaining wall of the ancient Jewish Temple in Jerusalem is 'stuffed' with prayers.

Reading the Guru Granth Sahib in a British gurdwara.

A Hindu woman making puja at home in Gujarat, India.

A Muslim father and sons praying at home in Britain.

'Let your mind settle like a clear forest pool'

Jack Kornfield is a Buddhist teacher and psychologist. He has developed this 'sitting meditation' and five other meditations for understanding and peace in everyday life.

To begin meditation, select a quiet time and place. Be seated on a cushion, taking an erect yet relaxed posture. Let yourself sit upright with the quiet dignity of a king or queen. Close your eyes gently and begin by bringing a full, present attention to whatever you feel within you and around you. Let your mind be spacious and your heart be kind and soft.

As you sit, feel the sensations of your body. Then notice what sounds and feelings, thoughts and expectations are present. Allow them all to come and go, to rise and fall like the waves of the ocean. Be aware of the waves and rest seated in the midst of them. Allow yourself to become more and more still.

In the centre of all these waves, feel your breathing, your life-breath. Let your attention feel the in-and-out breathing wherever you notice it, as coolness or tingling in the nose or throat, as a rising or falling of your chest and abdomen. Relax and softly rest your attention on each breath, feeling the movement in a steady, easy way. Let the breath breathe itself in any rhythm, long or short, soft or deep. As you feel each breath, concentrate and settle into each movement. Let all other sounds and sensations, thoughts and feelings continue to come and go like waves in the background.

After a few breaths, your attention may be carried away by one of the waves

of thoughts or memories, by body sensations or sounds. Whenever you notice you have been carried away for a time, acknowledge the wave that has done so by softly giving it a name such as 'planning', 'remembering', 'itching', 'restless'. Then let it pass and gently return to the breath. Some waves will take a long time to pass, others will be short. Certain thoughts or feelings will be painful, others will be pleasurable. Whatever they are, let them be.

At some sittings you will be able to return to your breath easily. At other times in your meditation you will mostly be aware of body sensations or of plans or thoughts. Either way is fine. No matter what you experience, be aware of it, let it come and go, and rest at ease in the midst of it all. After you have sat for twenty or thirty minutes in this way, open your eyes and look around you before you get up. Then as you move try to allow the same spirit of awareness to go with you into the activities of your day.

The art of meditation is simple but not always easy. It thrives on practice and a kind and spacious heart. If you do this simple practice of sitting with awareness every day, you will gradually grow in centredness and understanding.

Jack Kornfield, *Buddha's Little Instruction Book*, Bantam Books, 1994

Somehow I was different: a Charismatic Christian experience

'Charisma' means the 'gift of the spirit' and Charismatic Christians are 'in touch with the spirit' and allow themselves to be the 'channels' of the spirit. They are not a church organisation, as such, but a movement across many Christian churches. One member of this movement is Amy Davies, whose Christian faith began when she attended an evangelical rally.

I didn't really want to go to this rally. I knew what it was all about but my friends from school were going and so I thought: well, it can't do any harm. I'd been a bit unhappy recently, what with one thing and another, and I must've thought it could help me make some sense of my situation. So I was interested but a bit sceptical. I'd heard a lot about these American preachers and their methods.

The service began with singing. The music wasn't what I'd expected. There was a band and it was noisy. There seemed to be a lot of people there who were already Christians. You could tell by the way they were singing with enthusiasm… I'm not quite sure now what the preacher actually said but whatever it was it all seemed to make sense to me. He told us that the world was in a mess – well, I agreed with that. He told us many people's relationships were in a mess – well I definitely agreed with that. Then he said that Jesus

understood all of that and the reason he died was to mend broken relationships – well, I wasn't sure of that…

At the end he asked us to stand up and come to the front if Jesus had spoken to us during the service. I wasn't sure if what I was feeling was real and not just in my mind, so we came home. But somehow I was different. I'd decided in my own mind to follow Jesus and I suppose it was from that day onwards that I became a Christian.

I joined the church where my friends go and it meets in a school hall – not like a traditional church building. The worship wasn't quite what I expected, either. We have keyboards, drums and guitars. I like this kind of worship and the friendliness of the people in the church. Our worship isn't always noisy, happy-clappy stuff: there are moments of total quiet, too. Being a Charismatic church, there's a lot about the work of the Holy Spirit and one way it comes out in us is when we speak in tongues, because we follow Jesus.

I love our church because there's a real sense that God is there. We feel his presence every day and every time we meet together. I just wish more people could feel that. Some people say all we do is sing and pray but that's not true. The church is involved in all sorts of community projects. Last year, a group of us went to Bosnia and worked in a children's hospital. We organise a weekly club for senior citizens and our church has one of the largest youth clubs round here.

Joyous thanksgiving in Christian worship.

I and I: Rastafari words and worship

We Negroes believe in the God of Ethiopia, the everlasting God – God the Father, God the Son and God the Holy Ghost, the one God of all ages. That is the God in whom we believe, but we shall worship Him through the spectacles of Ethiopia… one day God and His hosts shall bring Princes out of Egypt and Ethiopia shall stretch forth her hands…

Marcus Garvey in *The Philosophy and Opinions of Marcus Garvey*, Amy Jacque-Garvey, Arno Press, 1969

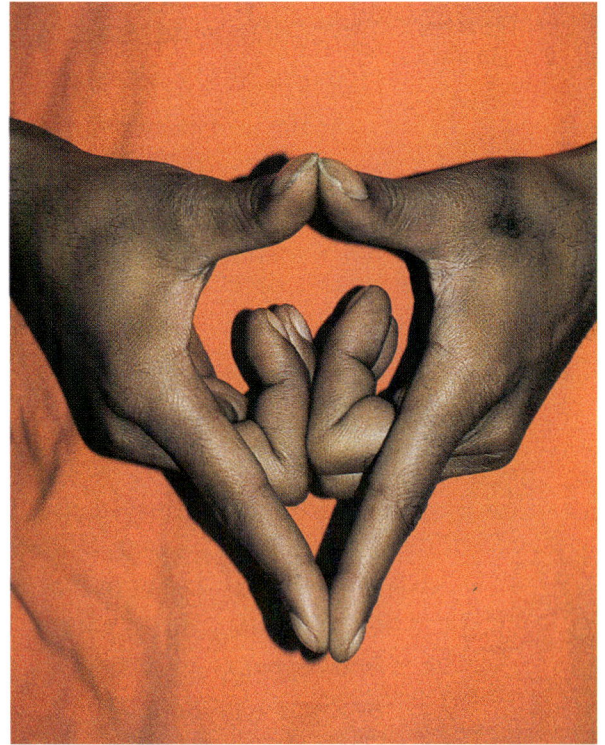

A Rasta with his hands in the symbolic heart and sword position.

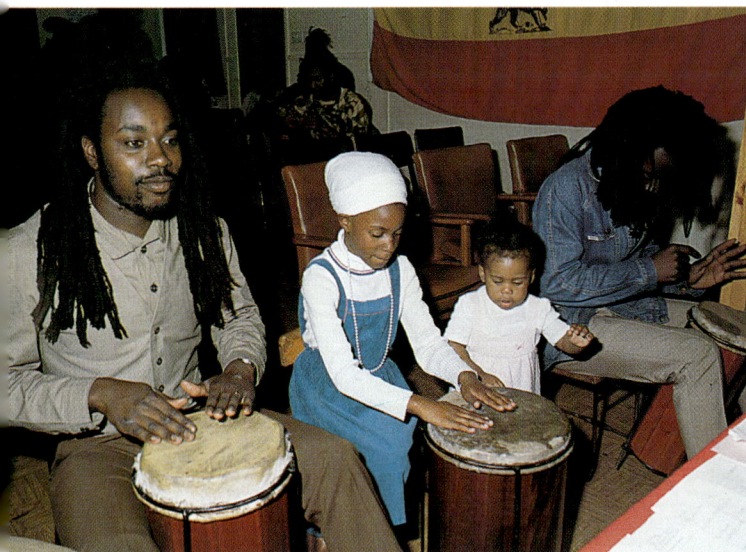

Rastas drumming in a service of worship.

For centuries in the Americas, African slaves who had become Christian heard Bible stories and saw that the Jewish people's experiences of slavery and exile were like their own. Most of them became disillusioned with white society and their low status within it. Their feeling that they really belonged to Africa – from where they had been taken by force – grew strong.

At the beginning of the 20th century, Marcus Garvey became an influential leader and prophet of black people in Jamaica, whose ancestors had been slaves. Many of them still suffered extreme poverty and prejudice. Marcus Garvey played a big part in the development of **Rastafari**: it grew slowly as a different way of looking at black people's experience and situation, and of recovering a sense of worth and a feeling of hope. Most **Rastas** (followers of Rastafari) say that Rastafari began in 1930 when Ras Tafari was crowned Emperor Haile Selassie I of Ethiopia, King of Kings, Lord of Lords, Conquering Lion of the

Tribe of Judah. He claimed to be a direct descendant of the Jewish king, David, through King Solomon and the Queen of Sheba. He excited many Jamaicans who were hoping for the Messiah to return.

Language is an important part of Rastafari life and worship. In everyday speech, they often use words like 'dispensation', 'fullness' and 'hellfire' which they have heard from the Bible, and they sometimes use words from Amharic (the Ethiopian language). They often say that 'wordsound is power' – an idea which comes from a passage in the Bible that, for them, describes Ras Tafari:

> *His eyes were as a flame of fire, and on his head were many crowns; and he had a name written that no one knew but he himself. And he was clothed with a vesture dipped in blood: and his name is called The Word of God... And out of his mouth goes a sharp sword, that with it he should strike the nations...*
>
> Revelation 19: 12, 13, 15

For Rastas, the most important and powerful letter of the alphabet is 'I' and it is also used as a number and a word. 'I' is part of Haile Selassie's title and the last letter of the word 'Rastafari'. But Rastas never just say 'I': they say 'I and I' and so include the presence and the divinity of God within themselves. 'I and I' also means the **bredren** (brethren, that is, other Rastas) and so includes all their members within each one of them. So 'I and I' is individual, social and holy. They also say 'I' with other words and substitute it for other letters, for example, 'I-ower' (power) and 'I-tal' (total).

Rastas also change words that have a negative meaning and have no hope in them. They would never say, 'I and I are going back' but rather 'I and I are going forward'. They do not say 'understand' but 'overstand' because 'under' is low.

When Rastas are talking to each other, they often say 'seen' as they nod in agreement or 'overstanding'. 'Seen' is a way of saying 'I and I know what you mean'. It is as if the words spoken are there in some physical way and have been completely accepted and 'overstood'. A long, deep conversation is called 'reasoning' because, by using their thoughts and expressions in a group, Rastas feel they are sharing an experience together – on any subject. When they greet and take leave of each other, at any time, they might say, 'Peace and love, Rasta' or 'Praises due Selassie I'.

Rasta men, women and children at a cantashun ('cantation') in Britain.

Many Rastas are natural poets, and every sentence, every thought, is expressed with rhythm, depth and gestures that emphasise, in sound and measure, the meaning. In the temples of the Almighty Ras Tafari Selassie I, the bredren, sisters and daughters chant their praises to Jah (God), and the chanting rises so powerfully, so harmonically, that once over, it seems to linger through any silence, beyond any dusk or dawn. Rastas bring great drama to their speech as they intone passages from the Bible... Which is what Rasta wants – to feel the power and strength of connection to Creation – which allows Rasta to be perceived by himself and others as worthy, as holy... Through their word-sounds, Rastas create their power.

Tracy Nichols, *Rastafari: A Way of Life*, Anchor Books, 1979

Questions and activities

1 Look at the spread of pictures on pages 16–17. Match each of the following phrases that describe aspects of worship to one or more picture:

A an individual praying or meditating alone

B a family at worship

C using texts in worship

D using an artefact or special things in worship

E being light-hearted

F being serious

G worshipping in a special place

H worshipping anywhere

I wearing special clothes for worship

J wearing everyday clothes for worship

K moving in a special way

L being still in worship

M moving in worship

2 Read 'Let your mind settle like a clear forest pool' on pages 18–19.

A What do you think is meant by:

'…an erect yet relaxed posture.'

'Let your mind be spacious and your heart be kind and soft.'

'Allow yourself to become more and more still.'

'Let the breath breathe itself…'

'The art of meditation is simple but not easy.'

'…you will gradually grow in centredness…'

B What do you think is the value of a 'sitting meditation' like this? Could anyone do it – whatever they believe, whatever their personality is like? Does it help to have 'instructions' or 'guidance'?

3 Look at and talk about all the different examples of worship in this chapter. How would you sum up 'worship'?

3 Ripples in the Pond

This chapter is about:

- the contrast between stillness and movement
- stillness and movement in worship
- the significance of meditation, particularly within Buddhism
- dance, story-telling and worship in the Hindu tradition
- the experiences of Charismatic Christians
- Islam – pattern, stillness and movement

Inside and outside

Have you ever thrown a stone into a completely still pond and watched the ripples spread outwards? The stone is lifeless. It has sunk to the bottom and stopped moving long before the ripples ebb away… Sometimes we can be busy on the inside and still on the outside, like when we're concentrating on a problem and hardly moving at all – while our minds are racing madly! Or we can feel still on the inside and busy on the outside, like when we're exercising frantically and repetitively and our minds blank out in a way… Do you ever get really agitated inside when you have to keep still? And do you ever find that doing something really energetic – like dancing or playing sports – makes you feel really calm?

Peter works in a factory on a production line, and writes poetry in his free time.

For one thing, I couldn't make a living out of writing poetry – and mine wouldn't exactly be a best seller! But anyway, I'd find it really hard just to sit all day and wait for inspiration, with a blank sheet of paper in front of me – getting blanker all the time! On the production line, I have to watch electronic components going down a tube and the machines are whirring all day long. We have ear plugs but they don't block out all the noise. The work is so mechanical that I feel like a machine myself. The good thing, though, is that it's so easy that I can switch off, and free my mind up to think what I like – and that's when I get poetical. I call it my 'poetry in motion'!

Alice remembers a particular science lesson when she was about 14.

We were doing something about wheels and motion, and measuring speed and distance. The teacher had this up-turned tricycle, with different-sized wheels, on the front bench and we were spinning the wheels at different rates. Then he said something that freaked me out – and still does. He told us that no matter how fast you spin the wheel, the centre doesn't budge. I said it must do: if the rim's going round the middle, the middle must be going round itself – or else it would break, wouldn't it? He said no, not really, because the middle isn't really there. It's just like a dot – it's infinitely small – and it's not really there. That's enough to blow your mind, that is.

Worship and meditation in all traditions have moments of stillness and movement – inwardly and outwardly.

Peace of mind

Maharishi Mahesh Yogi (right) with the Beatles, 1967.

Meditation is a way for someone to realise, or reflect on, a religious truth and to develop their spiritual life, but it is not always a religious practice. For example, some people today, who have no particular religion, practise Transcendental Meditation (TM) to find peace of mind. Many of them say that it gives them more energy and makes them work more efficiently. TM was brought to the West by Maharishi Mahesh Yogi in the late 1960s.

Maharishi (meaning 'Great Sage') Mahesh (his family name) Yogi ('one who has reached union with God') was born in India in 1911. When he was in his thirties, he retreated to the Himalayas for 13 years with his guru, to seek Enlightenment. His guru told him to evolve a single form of meditation for everyone. Maharishi formed a movement which became known as the Science of Creative Intelligence. With his simple white loincloth and beads, his rubber thonged sandals and always a flower in his hand, he became famous when the Beatles went to see him in the late Sixties.

Meditation – a path to Enlightenment in the Buddhist tradition

It is in the stillness of meditation that Buddhists most feel the movement of the world and aim to find their ultimate goal – Enlightenment. Meditation is something that anyone can practise: we have to train our mind and our whole being, to be free from the 'dis-ease' of life – the feeling of not being comfortable with life. Buddhists have different 'goals' for meditation and there are several types, or 'schools', of meditation in the Buddhist world today. All of them, however, come from the teaching of the Buddha who was a great teacher of meditation.

Each of the different hand positions of the Buddha are known as **muddas**. They each depict certain aspects of the Buddha's character.

The Noble Eightfold Path

The Eightfold Path is based on wisdom; kindness and fairness; and mental discipline. It is a practical guide to the end of suffering through a wise, helpful and thoughtful life. Buddhists do not take the steps of the Eightfold Path in order or even one at a time but try to live by all of them. They are like eight spokes on a wheel that are all equal and joined at the centre. The eight-spoked wheel has become a symbol for Buddhism.

1 *Right understanding:* seeing the world as it really is; understanding that living beings suffer and everything changes.
2 *Right thought:* having a pure mind and heart so that kind thoughts can grow.
3 *Right speech:* not lying, gossiping or saying anything that will lead to hatred or cruelty.
4 *Right action:* not killing or harming living things, stealing or making others unhappy; doing what you know to be right and helping others.
5 *Right livelihood:* living and working kindly and fairly.
6 *Right effort:* trying to remove bad thoughts and attitudes, and develop good thoughts and attitudes.
7 *Right mindfulness:* being constantly aware of our bodies and our mind.
8 *Right concentration:* training our minds to concentrate and see things clearly.

Right Concentration

A Buddhist nun describes 'right concentration' like this:

During meditation, we learn to drop from the mind what we don't want to keep. We only want to keep in our mind our meditation subject. As we become more and more skilled at it, we start to use the same faculty in our daily lives to help us drop thoughts which are unwholesome. In this way, our meditation practice assists us in daily living and our attention to wholesome everyday life helps our meditation practice.

Ayya Khema, *Being Nobody, Going Nowhere*, Wisdom Publications, 1987

Buddhists meditating in a temple in Myanmar, Burma.

Breath

Any of our actions – for example, walking, eating and breathing – can be the focus for meditation, of becoming awake to ourselves and the world around us. For Buddhists the breath is a good way to focus on the mind, because it is not something we normally think about, and yet it is the basis of life.

A young Buddhist describes how he controls his breath:

> *I first feel my breath passing through my nostrils, and coming up out of my chest. As I breathe slowly, I feel the cycle of my breath. In my head, I count the in-breath and the out-breath – up to 10. At the end of each cycle, I chant a word – usually 'Buddha' – which helps me think about Enlightenment. I need to **concentrate** rather than just think – and counting helps. To start with it was difficult – my mind kept wandering – but now I'm getting much better. It helps me to be more tranquil in my mind and much more relaxed. Some of my friends notice the difference in me. I used to worry about everything, but now I feel much more able to accept things as they are. I'm not saying I've got there yet. I've got a long way to go to achieve Buddhahood!*

Mettabhavana

There are several forms of Buddhist meditation and some need a great deal of self-discipline. Buddhist meditation is *self-centred* but is not *selfish* because it must also be 'a blessing to the world'. This idea is known as **metta**, or universal loving kindness. Mettabhavana is a widely practised form of meditation and has five stages:

1 Loving kindness (metta) towards ourselves. This means realising that we have the capacity to be loving to another person. 'May I be well, may I be happy, may I progress.'
2 Extending metta to a friend.
3 Extending metta to someone we don't know.
4 Extending metta to someone we dislike.
5 Finally, bringing these different people together and extending metta to all the world.

Some sayings of the Buddha

When you eat, eat slowly and listen to your body. Let your stomach tell you when to stop, not your eyes or your tongue.

Whatever we cultivate in times of ease, we gather as strength for times of changes.

Don't keep searching for the truth, just let go of your opinions.

To meditate is to listen with a receptive heart.

Stay centred, do not over-stretch. Extend from your centre, return to your centre.

No one outside us can rule us inwardly. When we know this, we become free.

Do not judge yourself harshly. Without mercy for ourselves, we cannot love the world.

When you meditate, sit with the dignity of a king or queen; when you move through your day, remain centred in this dignity.

Let your mind become clear like a still forest pool.

Those who are awake live in a constant state of amazement.

Jack Kornfield, *Buddha's Little Instruction Book*, Bantam Books, New York, 1994

The dance of life – dance and devotion in the Hindu tradition

In the Hindu tradition, dance is an important part of devotion to God. Some of the dance forms go back as far as 2500 years. The major traditional dance form is called **Bharata Natyam**. This is so complex that every movement is taught for limbs, hands and body, and there are as many as 36 instructions for glances.

A male dancer of the Kathakali tradition.

A female dancer of the Bharata Natyam tradition.

Other forms of Hindu dance:
- **Kathakali** – a dance form used for retelling the stories of the Hindu epics, such as the Ramayana and the Bhagavad Gita.
- **Kathak** – a strongly rhythmic dance which has accelerated foot tapping and dramatic turns.
- **Manapuri** – a dance which is almost acrobatic and full of vigorous movement.

All of these dances have their origins in the Hindu temple and are important parts of the devotion of the whole person to God.

Filled with the Spirit

Worship in the Pentecostal Church is spontaneous, lively and free. Sometimes people are so overwhelmed by God's Holy Spirit that they almost faint, and fall to the floor. This is known as being 'slain in the Spirit'. Closely linked to this tradition are **Charismatic Christians** who may belong to a well-established church or to a more informal group that meets, as the first Christians did, in people's homes ('House Churches'). 'Charisma' means the gift of the spirit.

Many Pentecostal Christians have the 'gift of prophecy': they can 'hear' God's voice and say what it means. Many 'speak in tongues'. To outsiders, it sounds like a jumble of sounds, but other members of the Church can often understand it. Language experts say that speaking in tongues is a human language – with its own vocabulary, grammar and intonation. Some say that perhaps we all have this language inside us but in only certain people does it find a voice. One young Christian woman has described it as 'being able to pray with my whole being, not just limited to the words of English.'

Being 'slain in the Spirit' at a healing and preaching service in the USA.

Roy Kerridge describes a service of worship where many prophecies were being received.

We waited our turn and listened to the other prophecies taking place… Moses the Scribe hovered here and there, waiting for a prophecy to emerge so he could record it on specially-printed prophecy paper. 'You won't have to wait long! Here is Prophetess Porritt now,' Father Peter encouraged us… 'Oh no! I've done seven prophecies tonight already!' Sister Porritt complained, in a Cockney accent. 'Surely someone else can do these two! My power is used up – this is ridiculous! Oh well, all right then.'

Taking a burning candle wrapped in palm fronds, she kneeled by my side and concentrated deeply. 'Nn-nn-noop! Noop! Noop! Noop!' she shrilled, then fell into a trance and spoke in guttural tones. 'The person behind the Prophetess-tess-tess-tess! Not this man – the person behind the Prophetess-tess!' As she herself was the Prophetess, the Spirit was speaking, not herself. It may have had to jerk itself out of her reluctant lips… The real seeker for knowledge was the young man, the person behind the Prophetess. 'No, no – the man beside you!' Moses anxiously corrected it.

I kneeled, almost curled up, with my blue and white tin plate and wobbling candle, as Prophetess Porritt absently traced patterns on my head with one finger. Impatiently, the spirit barked out a message in faulty gramophone needle-language, then dismissed me. 'You do not, do not, do not – need to worry, worry, worry. Your path will, path will, path will – be made clear, ear, ear, ear.'

… In due course, Moses handed me my Prophecy, hand-written on lined paper with a printed heading: 'Notes of Spiritual Revelation'… The prophecy covered four sheets of paper, each signed at the foot by Moses. Here are some extracts:

Listen to the voice of God to my son: the Lord is saying to you that He is able to do all things. I am the Lord that solves all problems. The Lord is saying to you, whenever you undertake any venture, first ask him… you are his son, and whenever you want anything, you know how to ask him. Never be worried unnecessarily. Many things have to be shown to you in dreams. Pray for recalled memories. Never doubt your dreams. They are true dreams from me, your Lord God. Ask for my divine protection in all your travelling. God's angels are with you — you are not alone. Peace be unto you, my son. (Written by Moses)

Who could fail to be pleased by such a prophecy?

Roy Kerridge, *The Storm is Passing Over*, Thames and Hudson, 1995

Islam – pattern, stillness and movement

For Muslims, as for so many other people, the idea of God is beyond human understanding. They see Allah as the Creator of the universe and every composition or creation owes its creativity to Allah. There can be no pictures or statues of Allah, who has no form ('body'). Yet Muslim artists,

Calligraphy, interwoven with repeating geometric and swirling floral patterns, on the walls of a mosque in Isfahan.

for centuries, have reflected the design of the universe in intricate and carefully constructed patterns. Many are symmetrical, suggesting close structure and order… and self-repeating, expressing infinity… and sometimes swirling and energetic, reflecting the energy of life.

The **hajj** (pilgrimage to Makkah) is a very personal journey and yet it is performed with millions of people. One **hajji** (male pilgrim) talks about the inner experience, amid swirling crowds:

Muslim pilgrims encircling the Ka'bah on hajj.

As I approached the Ka'bah, the holiest spot in Islam, my heart started thumping. Here I am, alone yet surrounded by so many – the moment I've waited for all my life. As we circle the Ka'bah, thoughts rush through my mind. Am I really here? Am I worthy of this? Tears come to my eyes as the sheer emotion of the occasion takes over me. So many thoughts – with only one thing I can say beyond the tears. Words come out, first in a stutter, then with great fervour:
'Allahu Akhbar' – God is Great.
'Allahu Akhbar' – God is Great.

Questions and activities

1 Watch a television programme – any programme – but plays, films, soap operas or sports matches are best for this.

   A Look carefully at the performers' or players' 'stillness' and 'movement'. On the whole, are they more 'moving' or more 'still'? Why do you think this is?

   B What thoughts and feelings are they showing by their actions and inaction? Write down or sketch about ten different examples and beside each one say what it shows.

   C Sometimes actions that show thoughts and feeling are called 'body language'. What do you think 'body language' means?

2 Read what Peter and Alice say on page 27. Try to sum up their ideas about stillness and movement.

3 Spend a few minutes listening to the cycle of your own breath. Write down your thoughts after you have done this. Then answer the following questions:

   A Why do Buddhists see meditation as important?

   B Why is concentration important?

   C What are the five stages of Mettabhavana?

4 Read 'Some sayings of the Buddha' on page 31.

   A Choose the saying that means most to you and talk about it with a partner.

   B Remember a time in your life when that saying was or could have been wise and true for you or someone you know.

   C *Either* describe the situation and say why the saying is wise and true.
      Or create a cartoon or other picture to show what the saying could mean.

5 In the Bible, read Acts 2: 1–21 carefully. It is about something that happened to Jesus' disciples (after he died) on the festival of Pentecost. Check the meaning of any words you do not know.

   A Join with a partner or a small group and share re-telling the story. What is the 'stillness' and what is the 'movement' in the story?

   B Match the account of the event with the description of Pentecostal worship on pages 34–35. What similarities and differences do you find?

   C Explain clearly why you think Charismatic Christians call themselves that?

   D 'Charisma' and 'charismatic personality' are often used in everyday language to describe someone who has a powerful effect or influence on other people, especially groups and crowds. Think of someone you know who has been described in this way. How does it compare with having a 'gift of the spirit'?

6 Look closely at the Islamic patterns on page 36.
   Either draw a similar pattern, with continuous lines and repeating shapes.
   Or think about the way that you see life and create a pattern to express your own view of the world.

4 Doing and Being

This chapter is about:

- the balance between what we do and who we are
- how religious traditions balance 'outer doing' and 'inner being'
- 'doing' and 'being' in the Jewish tradition
- an interview with Christian Aid
- sewa (service) in the Sikh tradition
- skilful and unskilful actions in the Buddhist tradition

Inner being and outer doing

We are social beings. We interact with our physical environment and we relate to other humans. These relationships are affected by how we are within ourselves. Our inner self and our outer life are linked.

Today's world is very demanding. We feel the pressure to be busy and to do something all the time. Sometimes it's like an addiction. Sometimes our 'doing' benefits ourselves and others but sometimes it is harmful. Doing something, whether positive or negative, helps us feel in control of our lives, that we matter as individuals, and can make a little stir in the endless activity of the world.

Look at the scenes in the pictures opposite. Which actions benefit others and which cause others harm? Do you think a person's actions show whether that person is 'good' or 'bad'?

*We're often so busy doing that we forget how to just **be**. We tend to put all our energies into acquiring new skills, reaching new goals and leading active lives, that we don't develop the ability to be still. For most of us, being inactive means being lazy or apathetic! That is a kind of 'being' that doesn't benefit anyone, least of all ourselves. But 'being' can also have a positive energy of its own, for example, when we stop racing around long enough to re-charge our batteries. It might be a moment of quiet reflection, when we're in touch with all our senses, or when we allow ourselves time to be creative and imaginative.*

Think for a moment: when was the last time you sat quietly and listened to the noises of the world around you, or felt the wind on your face, or saw shapes in the clouds?

To do is to be and to be is to do

For most religions, *being* and *doing* are closely related because each of us is a whole person, with a connected mind, body and spirit. Religions value stillness, self-examination and contemplation, but also teach that human beings should develop and use their talents, skills and initiative in practical ways. All religions emphasise a person's *intentions* in their actions: the outer doing – the activities that benefit others – are important but the inner intention matters as well. We need to think carefully before we act, to know why we are doing something before we do it.

Doing and being in the Jewish tradition

This story is set in a Jewish community in eastern Europe in the 19th century.

If Not Higher...

One year, just before the High Holy Days, a traveller arrived in a small Jewish community. He only meant to stay a few days and then move on. Early each morning, he prayed in the synagogue with everyone else and heard the ram's horn being blown, as it was each day before the Jewish New Year. He was very surprised that the rabbi was never there and when he asked people where he was, they always said, 'The rabbi's in heaven.'

Finding this a bit hard to believe, he decided to see for himself what the rabbi got up to so early each morning. Each evening and morning, the rabbi held study sessions in his home and one evening, when everyone left, the traveller hid under the rabbi's bed. Just before it got light, the rabbi got up, put on rough working clothes, picked up a length of rope and an axe, and left the house – with the traveller following at a safe distance.

Soon the rabbi reached a clearing in the forest, where he chopped some fallen trees into firewood, tied the sticks into a bundle and headed back. He stopped at a broken down house and tapped on the door. 'Hello,' the rabbi said, 'It's the woodcutter!' and went inside.

Peering through the window, the traveller saw a frail old woman lying on a bed, too feeble to get up. The rabbi put the wood in her stove, quietly reciting the first part of the morning prayers. The rabbi lit the wood, and said the second part, and as it caught fire, he said the third part. Then he left.

The rabbi hurried home and arrived just as the dawn was breaking and the sound of the ram's horn was piercing the morning air. He slipped into his house by the back door. By the time the congregation came out of the synagogue and arrived for morning study, he had changed into his normal clothes and was sitting at his desk with a book open in front of him.

The traveller was so impressed and so moved that he stayed for the High Holy Days, and eventually made his home there. From time to time, other visitors would pass through the village and they would also wonder, 'Where's the rabbi?' The members of the community would still reply, 'The rabbi's in heaven.' And the traveller would always add 'If not higher…' ■

Doing: a Jewish response to the needs of others

The Jewish tradition teaches that people are God's partners in the world. Some of God's actions can be performed by human beings. In Hebrew these are called **gemilut hasadim** which can be translated as 'acts of loving kindness'. The rabbis say that just as God gave clothes to the naked, visited the sick, comforted the grieving and buried the dead, so should the Jewish people also perform these acts of loving kindness, reflecting God's love for each other and for all humanity.

A day centre and workshop for elderly people in Jerusalem. There they have other people to be with and they can use and develop their skills.

A Jewish organised demonstration in London to protest against the abuse of human rights in Bosnia.

Tzedakah

Tzedakah is an important Jewish idea and action, sometimes translated as 'justice'. Tzedakah is far more than giving money to charity, or even compassion. It means getting personally involved in trying to put right something that is wrong in society, and using personal effort so that the world's goods are used for the good of humanity as a whole.

The Jewish tradition emphasises the idea that God often meets people's needs through other people's good actions. For Jews, the whole world belongs to God and it is their duty to share what they have. There is no shame in receiving tzedakah. One saying goes: 'The motto of life is: "Give and Take". Everyone must be both a giver and receiver. Who is not both is like a barren tree.'

Jewish charitable funds and donations are used for:

- Jewish organisations, such as schools or homes for the elderly
- housing and land development projects in Israel
- local or world-wide appeals, such as famine relief or medical care

Being: prayer and contemplation in the Jewish tradition

Any one of us could help other people, lead a good life, or even pray regularly without thought or understanding. For Jews, however, concentration and devotion are important parts of carrying out a **mitzvah** (commandment). The Hebrew word 'kavanah' means total concentration on what you are doing and participating *inside* yourself. The rabbis said that people should act as if they feel they were always in the God's presence. Rabbi Nachman of Bratslav said:

> '*It is impossible to be a good Jew without devoting each day a portion of the time to commune alone with God, and to have a conversation with God from the heart.*'

Some Jewish mystics have said that prayer should be a window to heaven. If there is kavanah in prayer, heaven and earth kiss, and God and people speak with each other. Prayer is the means of coming closer to God.

Silence gives us time to listen to the voice inside us. Some Jews sway as they pray. It helps them to get into the prayer and to pray with their whole body, their whole being.

A Jewish woman lighting Shabbat candles.

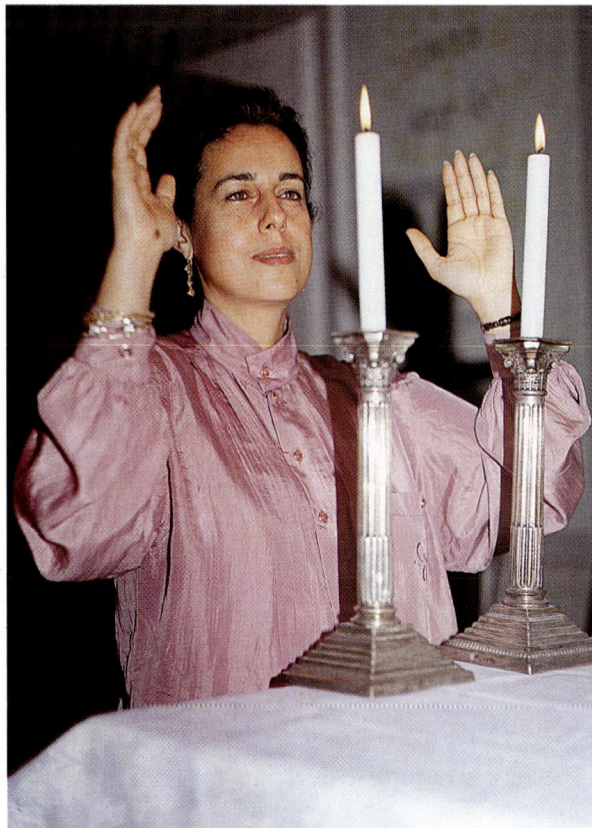

Hasidic Jews say that when someone prays with their whole heart, God will hear them. Their prayer is joyful and spontaneous song, and they often burst into song and dance. These men, at the Western Wall in Jerusalem are dancing in a traditional Hasidic style.

An interview with Christian Aid: a modern example of being and doing in the Christian tradition

Q What is Christian Aid all about ?

A Christian Aid is supported by churches of the UK and Ireland and it's a way for Christians to show their concern for the world's needs. Christian Aid sees the connection between being and doing, between belief and action.

*Q What is specifically **Christian** about Christian Aid's work?*

A Jesus was concerned about the poor, the sick and those living on the margins of society. We work with people who, for various reasons, have been pushed to the edges of today's society – especially people on low incomes who have nothing obvious to offer to society and no choice in what they do. So we see ourselves in line with Jesus' teaching about the outcasts of society.

We're not just about 'doing'. We're also about 'being'. Churches support Christian Aid's work with prayer and reflection, as well as practical help. This is particularly important when there's an international crisis: if we have a sense of hope and shared belief, we can cope better with the awful suffering that we see.

This is a picture of a family in Zimbabwe who belong to a community group supported by Christian Aid. The prayer on the back of the card shows how, for many Christians, prayer is a campaign along with other forms of practical involvement in the fight against injustice throughout the world:

*Spirit of God
Giver of life and love,
you tell the truth;
you burn away evil;
you require justice.
Set our hearts on fire
and make us one body
with all who seek your warmth.*

Q *What does Christian Aid actually do ?*

A *Many people, particularly if they're poor, have no say in their lives. Christian Aid helps them make choices and have a bigger voice in decisions that affect them. We support local groups in over 70 countries with funding, training and practical advice. We don't just go somewhere and set up programmes. Change has to come from a local group. The group brings its needs and ideas to Christian Aid and then we work through local churches and other organisations to help the group find its own solutions. Everyone must be included. For instance, we always look at the effect a project has on women, and try to make sure that they're involved all the way through.*

    If there's a major crisis, like a drought or an earthquake, we pool our resources with other big aid agencies – and provide food, water, clothing, shelter and medical supplies. We all work together to meet the people's needs and to make sure that the effect of any disasters in the future won't be so big. For instance, in Bangladesh Christian Aid helped to provide shelters and, when a cyclone hit the country, many people hid in those shelters and were safe.

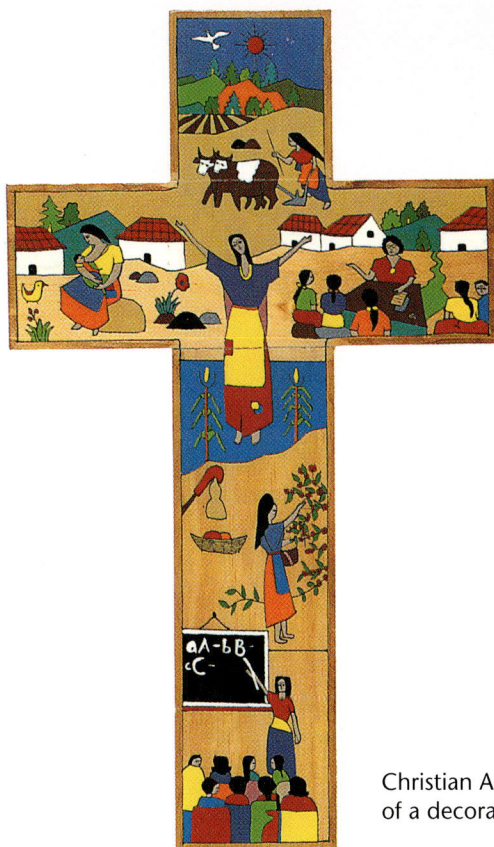

Q *Why does Christian Aid do educational work in the UK and Ireland?*

A *For one thing, because our partners in other parts of the world want it. Many decisions that affect the 'poor world' are made in the 'rich world' – and until the 'rich world' sees this, nothing will really change. People in the 'rich world' can influence decisions that affect the lives of people in the 'poor world'. Being a citizen of the world means more than going on a foreign holiday or learning another language. It's about understanding how everyone's connected. It means knowing something about the politics and trade – and acting on that so that it's fairer for everyone in the world.*

Christian Aid prayer card, in the form of a decorated cross, from Salvador.

Sewa

For Sikhs, doing and being are both important. The ideal of Sikh conduct is summed up as:

- **Nam japna:** always keep God in mind
- **Kirat karna:** work hard and honestly
- **Vand chhakna:** give to charity

Worship and meditation must be balanced with honest work and good deeds. The Sikh scripture says:

There can be no worship without performing good deeds.

Adi Granth 4

Guru Nanak talked about this balance when he said:

As the lotus in the pool and the water fowl in the stream remain dry, so a person should live untouched by the world.

It is hard to live like a beautiful lotus floating above a dirty pond – to live in the world with all that it offers and not be corrupted by it. The person who is God-conscious (gurmukh) does not give up on the world and go into retreat from it, but lives a full life as a 'trader in truth'.

In this gurdwara, homeless people regularly come to the langar to eat: for some of them, it is the only 'decent meal' they ever get.

When Sikhs speak of God as **Sat Nam** (Truth), they remember to be truthful in their thoughts, words and deeds. They also try to reflect other qualities of God, like love for everyone. Sikhs aim not just to become better people but to make society better, too. Humanity is one, and so everyone deserves to be treated with the same respect.

Sewa means service to others. Some acts of sewa are very ordinary, everyday expressions of devotion in the gurdwara, such as preparing or serving food in the langar, helping with repairs, welcoming visitors and strangers, looking after the shoes or giving out water to drink.

The langar, or communal kitchen, trains people in sewa. Everyone has the chance to help out, no matter how old or young, rich or poor, male or female. And everyone is treated the same. The langar emphasises the unity and equality of all people.

This is a popular story from the Sikh tradition. It shows the importance of treating all people with respect. God has no favourites.

Guru Nanak: Bread of Milk and Bread of Blood

One day, Guru Nanak and his travelling companion Mardana came to a town where they were welcomed by a carpenter called Bhai Lalo. He invited them to his house and shared his simple meal with them. Guru Nanak and Mardana stayed at Bhai Lalo's house for several days.

In the same town lived a wealthy man called Malak Bhago who invited all the other wealthy, famous people of the town to a banquet. He sent an invitation to Guru Nanak but he refused to go. Malak Bhago was angry and asked Guru Nanak why he wouldn't go – and why he preferred to eat with Bhai Lalo, a carpenter. Guru Nanak said, 'I'll show you why I didn't want to eat your food. Please, bring me some bread from your kitchen. And Bhai Lalo, please bring me some of the bread from your kitchen.'

Guru Nanak took Malak Bhago's fine bread in one hand and Bhai Lalo's coarse bread in the other, and squeezed both hands. From the fine bread came drops of blood but from the coarse bread came drops of milk. 'You see,' said Guru Nanak to Malak Bhago, 'Lalo's bread is the result of hard work and honest living, but yours comes from robbing and exploiting other people. That's why I wouldn't eat with you.' ▪

Skilful and unskilful actions in the Buddhist tradition

The Buddhist tradition teaches that everyone's actions during their life have consequences for them – immediately or later, directly or indirectly. Buddhists sometimes speak of actions as 'skilful' or 'unskilful' rather than 'good' or 'bad'. 'Skilful' actions bring peace, joy and wisdom. 'Unskilful' actions lead to anger, greed or ignorance. For Buddhists, the Buddha is the model of a 'skilful' person. Buddhists do not worship Buddha but think of him as an Enlightened being. When they meditate, they might use an image of the Buddha to recall his wisdom and compassion, and his virtuous life.

Buddhist monks in meditation.

We are what we think.
All that we are arises with our thoughts.
With our thoughts we make the world.
Speak or act with an impure mind
And trouble will follow you
As the wheel follows the ox that draws the cart.
We are what we think.
All that we are arises with our thoughts.
With our thoughts we make the world.
Speak or act with a pure mind
And happiness will follow you
As your shadow, unshakeable.

A saying of the Buddha from *The Dhammapada*

Questions and activities

1 Copy out the chart below, find the Bible references and complete the chart.

Bible reference	Who did God perform the 'act of loving kindness' for?	What was God's 'act of loving kindness'?
Genesis 3:21		
Genesis 18:1		
Genesis 25:1		
Deuteronomy 34:6		

2 Imagine that you are the woman in the story 'If Not Higher…' on pages 40–41 and you are later visited by a friend or relative. Tell him or her about what the rabbi did for you, and say what you think about it.

3 One of Christian Aid's slogans, which appears on their posters and in their leaflets, is 'We believe in life before death.' Talk about what that slogan means.
- *Either* write a poem on the theme of 'life before death'
- *Or* create a collage of pictures on the theme of 'life before death'
- *Or* write an article, fund-raising leaflet, or booklet for young children about Christian Aid, based on the information on pages 44–45.

4 Read the Sikh story 'Guru Nanak: Bread of Milk and Bread of Blood' on page 47.
A Present it as a cartoon strip.
B If you were Malak Bhago, how would you have responded to Guru Nanak at the end of the story?

5 Think and talk about the Sikh saying: 'As the lotus in the pool and the water fowl in the stream remain dry, so a person should live untouched by the world.' Write down as many examples as you can of people (famous or not) who live or have lived 'untouched by the world'.

6 Read the passage from *The Dhammapada* that starts 'We are what we think…' on page 48. Copy the passage out and make a poster by illustrating the images in the passage with your own drawings or cut out pictures. You might want to turn to page 12 for an idea of the way that an artist illustrates the images in a passage.

5 Yesterday, Today and Tomorrow

This chapter is about:

- the importance of change as a part of growing
- how traditions have changed
- tradition and change in Judaism
- the changing face of the Christian Mission

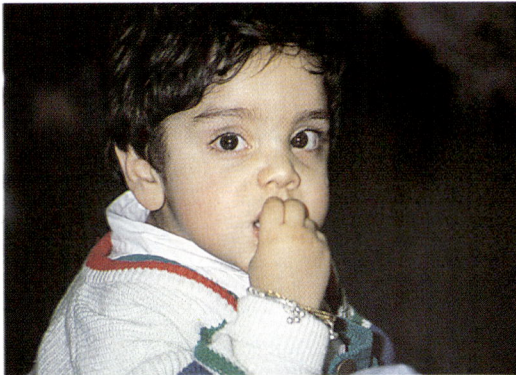

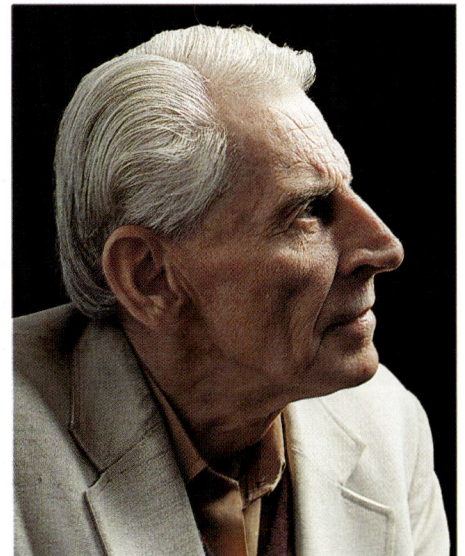

Changing and staying the same

Have you always been you? What were you like when you were a baby? What's different about you now? What has stayed the same? By the time this lesson has ended, you'll have aged. You will never be the same as you were at the beginning of the lesson. The change may not be noticeable immediately but it is happening.

Whole societies change, too – for good or for bad. What has changed in your community since you were younger? Elderly people, in particular, often look back to the days of their youth as if today isn't quite the same. They might say 'In our day…' or 'Things aren't what they used to be'. Sometimes people feel trapped by traditions and break out of them. Or they might still keep them even if they think they're 'out of date' – why do you think they do? Are there any traditions at school, for example, that you don't feel give you enough freedom?

Change in religious traditions

Religious groups vary in the way they see their traditions, how much they need to change and how far they are willing to change. There may be differences within a religious group, too. Some people think that certain things are so true that they cannot be questioned or changed. They may feel that children and young people have to be protected from different ideas. Others may feel that no one 'owns' truth and the more they are exposed to other experiences and ideas, the richer and fuller they are. Some people are in between these opposite views.

Tradition plays an important part in all religions, but usually develops slowly as believers explore and discover new ways of expressing their faith. Most believers feel they can do this without denying the eternal 'truths' and, those who belong in a changing tradition actually feel that it is in keeping with their tradition to change it.

Young Sikhs at a political demonstration in Britain. Some have uncut hair and turbans and some have cut their hair yet have covered it with a scarf.

Muslim girls in modern dress with head scarves during break at their Qur'an school.

Tradition and change – four stories

This Indian legend is about a tradition that develops for a particular reason but continues after the reason disappears. In time, quite different reasons are found for keeping the tradition.

The Guru's Cat

When the guru sat down to worship each evening, the ashram cat would get in the way and distract the worshippers. So he ordered that the cat be tied during evening worship. After the guru died, the cat continued to be tied during evening worship. And when the cat expired, another cat was brought into the ashram so that it could be duly tied during evening worship.

Centuries later, learned treatises* were written by the guru's scholarly disciples on the liturgical† significance of tying up a cat while worship is performed. ■

Anthony de Mello, *The Song of the Bird*, Doubleday, 1984

* Writings by scholars in which they explain complicated ideas.
† To do with ritual worship.

Nasruddin was a legendary mullah, an Islamic teacher, with a reputation for wisdom, for seeing things from an unusual point of view, and for a cheeky sense of humour.

Carrots

The King sent Nasruddin to find out about the ideas and customs of mystics in the East. The mystics all told him about the miracles and sayings of their ancient founders and teachers – all long dead. When Nasruddin came back, he submitted his report to the King which had only one word in it: 'Carrots'.

When the King summoned him to explain himself, he said: 'The best part is buried. Apart from the farmer, few people can tell from the green part that there is orange underneath. It's very healthy and nourishing. If you don't work for it, it will rot. And it's often connected with a lot of donkeys!' ■

The Buddha told this parable to show that we should not hang on to things which are no longer useful.

The Raft

Once a man on a long journey came to a river. He thought: it's dangerous and difficult to walk on this side of the river but it looks a lot easier on the other side. So he made himself a raft of branches and reeds, climbed on and paddled safely across. Then he thought: this raft has been very useful to me so I won't leave it to rot on the bank but I'll carry it with me. He continued on his journey, with the wet, heavy raft on his shoulders.

The Buddha asked: if he took on an unnecessary burden, can he be called wise? ■

This is a modern version of a story of Christian origin which is found in several countries. It is a parable about safety and security. It is also about the challenges of freedom and the need to take risks for the sake of love and growth.

The Wandering Sheep

A sheep found a hole in the hedge and scrambled through. He wandered far over the countryside and got very, very lost. There were wild rottweiler dogs around and they attacked and chased after the sheep. The sheep ran and ran, it was utterly petrified. The shepherd went out looking for the sheep, and found it. She fought off the dogs and carried the sheep lovingly back to the fold. 'You must repair the hedge,' people said to the shepherd. 'No,' she said, 'I cannot fence them in. I love my sheep too much.' ■

Angela Wood and Robin Richardson, *Inside Stories: Wisdom and Hope for Changing Worlds*, Trentham Books, 1992

'Renew the old and sanctify the new': traditional and modern Jewish life

Father   Richard   Paul   Ruth

The picture on the right shows a fairly traditional seder (Passover supper) in a British Jewish family. There are the parents, Miriam and David, four of their five children and other guests. The table is laid with ritual objects and symbolic foods.

The Jewish tradition dates back 4000 years and there are now Jewish communities all over the world: Jewish generations have lived in many situations and cultures, and have experienced many changes. Throughout, the Torah (teaching) which Jews received 3000 years ago has remained the same. Individuals and groups, however, understand it and apply it to their lives in different ways.

In Europe for over 1000 years, Jews were 'outsiders' in most Christian countries. They were shut off from the outside world and new ideas, but their closely-knit community helped them feel secure and helped tradition survive. In the last few centuries, Jews have become part of the 'open society'. Although they still face prejudice, they have many more opportunities for education, work, housing and for mixing with other people. This puts them in touch with new influences.

A question the Jewish people ask today is: what to keep and what to give up? Some Jews say nothing must change: Jewish life is so 'whole' that to lose a part of it would spoil it all. Some say customs can change but the essential teaching must never be allowed to die. Some say Jewish thinking became 'stiff' when it was closed off and lost touch with the heart of the Torah: they must return to that. Some just say Jews should take the best from the society in which they live – and give their very best to it.

Rabbi Jonathan Sacks (in *Traditional Alternatives: Orthodoxy and the Future of the Jewish People*) talks about the changes facing the Jewish community today. He takes an imaginary but 'typical' family: Miriam and David Cohen, and their five children. He uses the seder as the scene where they would all be together and the children's differences from their parents – and from each other – might be clear. At a seder, there are songs and readings from a haggadah ('telling') book which tells the story of the Jewish people's ancient escape from slavery to freedom. The haggadah speaks of four 'types' of children and how adults should treat them as individuals: the wise child, the wicked child, the simple child and the child who does not know how to ask. Rabbi Sacks calls them the 'intellectual', the 'rebel' the 'single-minded' and the 'child without questions'. To meet today's situation, he adds another that he just calls the 'fifth child'.

The Cohen family is warm and the children had a happy, secure childhood. The parents have always been Orthodox – that is, strictly traditional. When the children were young, they went to synagogue each Shabbat, but they go less often now. On Shabbat, they light candles, make kiddush and eat a traditional Shabbat meal but they often watch television, too. They keep a kosher (permitted) kitchen but sometimes eat in a non-kosher restaurant – though never meat. The parents don't cover their hair, except at the synagogue.

Each child relates to the Jewish tradition and their upbringing in his or her own way.

The Five Children

The Intellectual

Ruth is 23, intelligent and communicates well. Going to university was difficult as it was the first time she had non-Jewish friends. Some of their morals and values were new to her but she learned to live with this and enjoy their friendship. She now teaches in a Jewish secondary school. From an early age, she wasn't very happy about the compromises her parents made and listened very closely to her Jewish Studies teachers. She and her fiancé have decided that, when they get married, she'll cover her hair, as a sign of modesty, and their home will be strictly kosher. Ruth has stopped going to her parents' synagogue which is far too 'showy' for her. Hers is a converted old house where people pray and study seriously. Yet all is not well. Sitting behind the curtain in the women's section she feels, as a woman, a bit irrelevant. But she's chosen an Orthodox lifestyle and keeps her questions to herself. If things are not quite right, she will accept it, knowing it is what she has chosen.

The Rebel

Richard is 21 and has just finished university. He keeps his faith, but under protest, mainly to make his parents happy. He was always a bright child: by the age of ten, he was complaining that his Jewish School was irrelevant and boring, and he always used to argue with the rabbis. Now he sits at the seder table because it's 'the price you have to pay for having parents'. Given the chance, he would ditch his Jewish background but knows he never can: whatever happens, it's always a part of him. He is aware that, one day, he might change his mind but, for the moment, he wants as little to do with it as possible.

The Single-Minded Child

Before he started university Paul, aged 19, spent some time in Israel and decided to stay: he loves Israel and cannot wait to get back after Pesach. He knows it is a commandment (mitzvah) to honour his parents but feels they have grown apart and no longer speak the same language. He needs to supervise the kitchen, to make sure they meet the standards he now has, and feels the relaxed atmosphere of home takes him away from his thoughts about his faith. He is a 'baal teshuvah' (a 'master of returning') – someone who re-discovers the faith and tradition that they have somehow lost, or earlier generations lost. Using his Hebrew name, Pinchas, every day is a sign of this. He talks openly about the change in his life: it was God who brought him to this experience and he sees his past life as a case of 'mistaken identity'. He only reads religious books now and blames the world's problems on a lack of holiness. His parents' Jewish life is superficial and Ruth's is based too much on the intellect. The right path must involve prayer and a 'mystical' experience. His parents do not really understand his new lifestyle.

The Child without Questions

Susan, the youngest at 15, is still at school. She is just like any other teenager of her age – wearing the same fashions, listening to the same music and addicted to the same soap operas. She finds heavy talk about Judaism a bore. She is the only one who is prepared to go with her parents to the synagogue: she likes looking down at the boys from the ladies gallery! She wants to marry a Jewish boy with a good job, have a big car and a nice house. She would like to belong to a synagogue but not go there too often. Susan would say she is not religious, but does feel completely Jewish. She supports Israel and would not mind if her future children decided to live there. She belongs to a young Jewish fund-raising group. Ruth's and Paul's obsession with religion is too much: she would like to 'keep the faith' but not if it demands too much.

The Fifth Child

Avi is not at the seder. He knows exactly what being a Jew means: to settle and build a new home in Israel. He talks about 'leaving exile' and building a new society in Israel. He is very passionate about this and gets cross with his family, who every year as part of the seder say, 'Next year in Jerusalem' without ever meaning it. He sees the next stage of Jewish history as fighting to establish this land. For him, it is a political struggle. 'At the seder, we drink four cups of wine,' he says, 'but there is a fifth cup – for entering Israel.' In many ways he is like the fifth cup because he does not choose to ask questions about history but decides to make it happen.

Spreading the Good News – the changing face of the Christian Mission

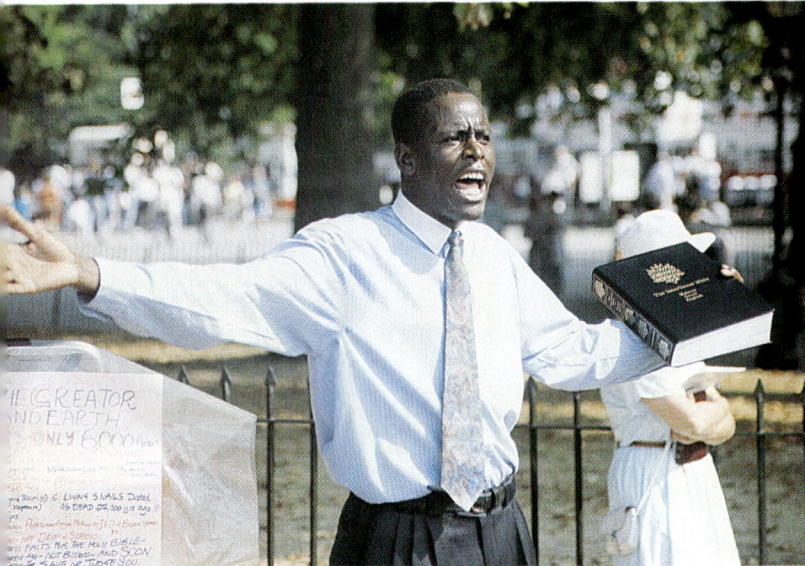

A black Evangelist preaching to crowds out of doors in Britain.

The heart of traditional Christian belief is that Jesus brought the Good News that the 'kingdom of God is at hand'. He made this possible by dying for the sins of the world, rising from the dead and ascending into heaven. In the decades after he died, early Christians wrote the **Gospels** 'through the eyes of faith': they tell many of the things that Jesus did and said, and how the early Christians understood them. 'Gospel' means 'Good News'.

Mission

When Jesus last saw his followers, he said to them:

> *Go, then, to all peoples everywhere and make them my disciples: baptise them in the name of the Father and of the Son and of the Holy Spirit, and teach them to obey everything I have commanded you. And remember! I will be with you always, to the end of the age.*
>
> Matthew 28: 19–20; Good News Bible

In the years and centuries that followed, Christians were inspired by the Good News and many obeyed Jesus' command to share it with others. Christianity spread by being 'taken' to new places and situations by Christian missionaries – rapidly to nearby countries in the first 100 years and in 'waves', in later centuries. There was a 'wave' of missionary activity by European explorers in the 15th and 16th centuries: missionaries from Spain and Portugal, for example, converted the peoples of central and south America to Christianity, often by force. They believed that the non-Christian world was 'heathen' and inferior, that non-Christians needed to be saved and that the Christian faith was a gift. They were influenced by the belief that there is no salvation outside the Church.

Victorian missionaries

In the 19th century, world trade expanded and the British Empire grew. Victorian missionaries, such as the famous Dr David Livingstone, were particularly active in Africa 'in the name of medicine and Christianity'. Medical missions brought health care from Europe and developed new medicines there, such as treatments for leprosy. They saw it as their mission to bring, not only the Christian message, but also Victorian values and customs. They did not wish to understand or appreciate the 'natives' – only to change them – and they branded them as 'heathen' and 'superstitious'. Under pressure from the Europeans, much of the local culture died out or was destroyed for ever.

A lithograph of a Victorian missionary preaching to African children.

Mission today

Most Churches today recognise that they need to work alongside people of different faiths, as well as people who have no religious faith, to make the world more caring and just. There is now more emphasis on 'training' than on 'treating' people and more respect for the people's culture. This is what a Western missionary in the Philippines says:

A Western medical missionary from the Elim Church.

I see my work as defending people who can't defend themselves – like children forced into prostitution or drug trafficking, or else sold abroad as 'mail-order brides', because they are the only ways to survive. We try to break the poverty trap by providing a basic education to better their chances. We try to 'empower' the women to be able to stand up for their rights. But it's hard for them because they know that, if they speak out, they might face terrible danger.

I don't see my role as trying to convert them. Quite the opposite! Some of them have a much greater understanding of God than I can ever hope to have. I'm sure it comes from their suffering. They have a much greater feel for the story of the crucifixion of Jesus than people in the West. I'm here to give them something of myself – but I'm privileged to learn so much from them.

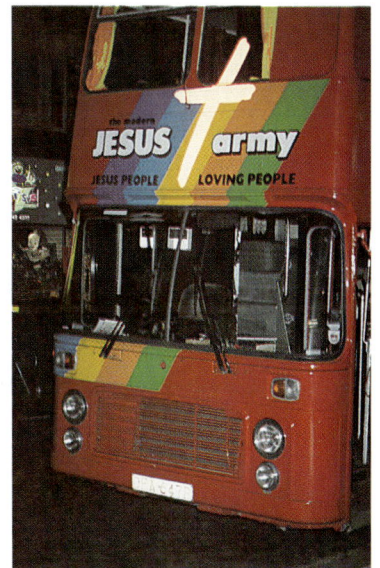

The Jesus Bus is a mission on wheels – with young British people in mind.

The Football Match – A Modern Parable

One day God came down from heaven and went to an important football match between the Yellows and the Purples.

For the first half, God dressed herself with the scarf, cap and emblem of the Yellow team supporters, and stood on the Yellow terraces. Three times during the first half, the Purples scored a goal. Each time the Purple team supporters jumped up and down, hugged each other, and waved their scarves and banners over their heads, from side to side. Some Yellow team supporters just stood there, silent and miserable. Others booed, jeered and taunted! But God leaped and shouted and waved with delight. The Yellow team supporters were very angry and some thought she must be mad.

For the second half, God dressed herself with the scarf, cap and emblem of the Purple team supporters, and stood on the Purple terraces. Three times during the second half, the Yellows scored a goal. Each time the Yellow team supporters jumped up and down, hugged each other, and waved their scarves and banners over their heads, from side to side. Some Purple team supporters just stood there, silent and miserable. Others booed, jeered and taunted! But God leaped and shouted and waved with delight. The Purple team supporters were very angry and some thought she must be mad.

In the amusement arcade after the match, some Purple and Yellow supporters happened to meet. God was in there, too, playing on one of the machines, and now wearing both sets of scarves, caps and emblems. Purple and Yellow supporters talked to each other about her, and said they thought she must be completely mad. 'I wonder,' said one of the supporters, 'what she thinks she's playing at!' ■

Questions and activities

1 Think about the changes in your life since you were born.
   A List the main changes, using a colour to mark those that are to do with your physical growth and development; a second colour to do with specific events that changed you (such as moving home); and a third colour for changes in society that shape the way you think and feel, and what you believe or value.
   B Draw a timeline for the changes in your life. You may like to use 'secret coding' for very personal events.
   C What do you find about the links between different types of changes.

2 Read the four stories on pages 52–53 ('The Guru's Cat', 'Carrots', 'The Raft' and 'The Wandering Sheep').
   A Talk about the meanings behind each one.
   B Choose *one* story that seems similar to a situation you, or someone you know, are in. How could you use the meaning of the story to understand that situation better?

3 Look at each of the 'five children' on pages 56–57.
   A What picture do they paint of Jewish society today?
   B How typical do you think each of them is of young people today?
   C Which 'child' do you find most in common with or agree with more? Why? ·
   D In a similar style, write your own descriptions to fit the beliefs represented in your class or other group.
   E Choose one of the children and imagine how their thinking and lifestyle will develop and change in the next few years. If he or she has children, how do you imagine they will be brought up?

4 Make a list of similarities and differences between the early missionaries, the Victorian missionaries and missionaries today.

5 Missionaries today often deal with injustices and speak up for those who do not have a voice. What opportunities would there be for missionaries in Britain to deal with injustices? What would their message be?

6 Read and talk about the modern parable 'The Football Match' on page 60.
   A How can you explain the behaviour of 'God'?
   B What is 'God playing at'? Do you agree that 'God must be mad'?
   C What points is the parable trying to make?

6 The Other Half

This chapter is about:

- what it means to be male and female
- the ordination of women in the Christian Church
- religious views of gender and sexuality
- Jewish ideas about sexuality

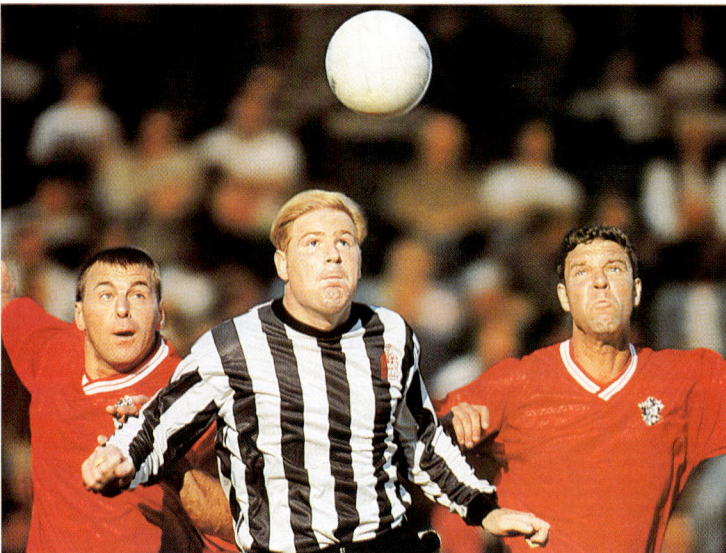

Men and women today

What do the pictures opposite and below show about the roles that men and women play in Western society? Has it always been like that – and is it completely like that now? Do you think men and women are 'equal'? And does 'equal' mean the 'same'? If you think men and women are different – not just in the way they look but deep down – what are those differences? Do you think any of your answers depend on whether you're male or female? We know that women's roles are changing in Western society and in many other societies, too. These changes are in their sexual behaviour, their work, the way children are brought up, and in many other aspects of their life. A woman and a man are both human, however, so one cannot change without the other changing – and without their relationship changing.

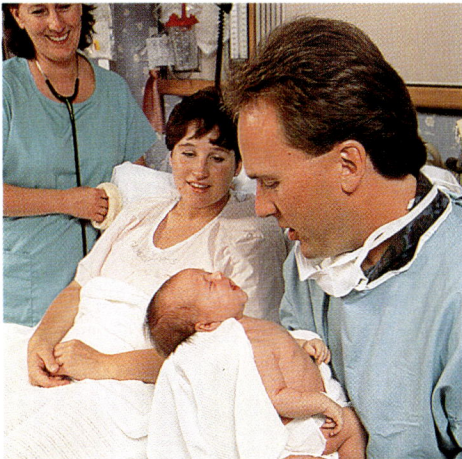

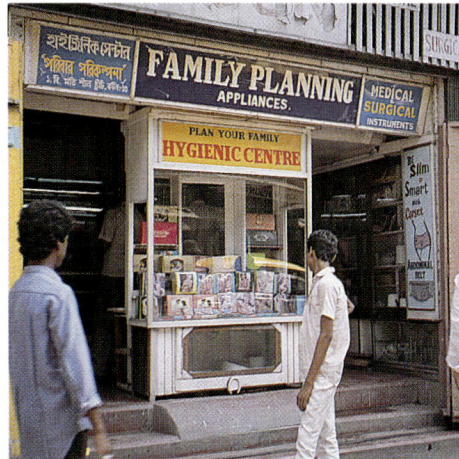

Most of the world's religions have seen men and women as having different characteristics, abilities and needs. Some traditions have said they are equal in different ways and, on the whole, they have seen women's strengths in family life and men's strengths in public life. The value of men and women, therefore, has partly been to do with the value the tradition places on the home and the community. Today, many religious traditions are re-thinking the way they see women's and men's roles, and the relationship between them: they may also be re-thinking the language they use for God. In many cases, God is described as 'he': that may be because there isn't one word for both 'he' and 'she', but it affects people's ideas of God just the same. In some traditions, God is sometimes 'she' or there are feminine aspects of God. Yet in other traditions, God is both male and female or neither male nor female.

Women in the Christian Church

In the Christian Church, thoughts about male and female images and roles have focused largely on the question of whether women can be priests. In the Roman Catholic and Orthodox Churches, and in some Evangelical Churches, only men can be priests. Protestant Churches do not have priests as such, but their ministers perform certain ceremonies, as well as teach and preach.

Traditionally in the Church of England, women could not be ordained as priests but they could be ordained as deacons, who carry out some, but not all, of the priestly functions.

Reasons for and against wome

AGAINST

1 'Christians mustn't break with the tradition of the Church which is based on what Jesus said and did.'

2 'There were many times when Jesus didn't go along with what people in his society said or did. So, even though women didn't have public leadership roles, he could have chosen women as his disciples and not worried what people thought. But he **didn't** choose women as his disciples so that must mean he doesn't want women to be priests.'

3 'Only a man can represent Christ at the altar because the incarnation (God becoming human) was to the male sex. In the New Testament, there are images of Christ as a bride **groom** and the Church as his bride. A priest represents the community only because he represents Christ first.'

4 'Paul talked about equality – everybody being at one in Christ through baptism. Women and men are **equal but different** in the eyes of God: God wants them to play different roles in the body of Christ.'

5 'It is the wrong time to ordain women because it would prevent union with other Churches that don't have women priests – like the Roman Catholic Church, the Orthodox Churches and many Evangelical Churches.'

In some countries, there have been Anglican women priests for several years – but not in Britain. Some Anglican women in Britain, who had a vocation to the priesthood, felt the Church was rejecting their calling. In the 1980s and early 1990s, in particular, this led to a lot of debate in the Church, including the General Synod (Council), about women priests.

An Anglican woman priest in Britain celebrating the Eucharist.

eing priests in the Christian Church

FOR

1. 'The Bible was written by and for a particular people at a particular time in the early Church. There are lots of issues we have today that the Bible doesn't deal with. So, just because Jesus only had male disciples, doesn't mean we can only have male priests in our society where women and men can have the same roles.'

2. 'Jesus challenged the idea that women were inferior to men. The reason he didn't have women disciples is that women didn't lead worship and didn't have authority to speak in public.'

3. 'The incarnation is about God becoming a **human** not about God becoming a male. If you say that Jesus' sex is important, you also have to say it is important that he was a Jew and from a poor family. Does that mean all priests have to be Jewish and poor, as well as male?'

4. 'The Church just shows women as submissive. The Bible, however, shows women in an active, positive way. So the Church should as well – and let them be priests!'

5. 'Christianity isn't just a religion of the book: it believes God is always involved with the world and is always revealing himself. If the spirit of God is calling women to be priests, then the Church has to listen.'

This is what some individual Christians – male and female, lay and ordained – said about the ordination of women:

'I couldn't cope with seeing a woman at the altar celebrating Communion. It would make me feel women are trying to be men.'

Sally, a lay Anglican

'The Church shouldn't be behind society: with its eternal truths, it should lead society. Why is the Church worrying about women priests? It should get on with ordaining them and spend more time dealing with other injustices, like poverty.'

Father Jim, an Anglican priest

'Women have a lot more to offer the Church than flower arranging and cleaning brass. It's important that the Church puts women's God-given gifts to good use. It needs them!'

Rachel, a lay Anglican woman

These are the headlines and captions from the national daily newspapers on Thursday 12 November, 1992 – the morning after the vote.

A GIANT STEP FOR WOMANKIND

Daily Mail

Anglicans go through the sex barrier

Daily Mail

Thank God for a silent majority

Daily Mail

Why the Church will never be the same

Daily Mail

Frock of Ages! Women can be vicars

Daily Mirror

Joy at Synod decision but Rome sees grave obstacle to unity

The Independent

Church say yes to their vicars in knickers

The Sun

Women win priesthood vote

The Independent

'They have finally admitted we are human too'

The Independent

'If we ordain women, we might as well throw the Bible away. Women are equal but different – and they shouldn't be priests. I'd feel very unhappy if I had to leave the Church I'm called to serve in but, if women were ordained, I'd feel I have to.'

Father David, an Anglican priest

'I feel called to serve God as a priest. I can lead worship but never consecrate the bread and wine. I know God doesn't judge me because I'm a woman but the Church does. I pray the time will come soon and I have faith that God will move us forward to that time. Meanwhile, I wait with hope!'

Mary, an Anglican women deacon

On 11 November, 1992, Mary's hopes were fulfilled when the General Synod of the Church of England voted to allow women to be ordained to the priesthood. Soon afterwards, Father David did what he sadly said he would: he left the Church.

Turmoil over Synod vote for women
The Daily Telegraph

Grave obstacle to unity talks, says Vatican
The Daily Telegraph

Joy at go-ahead for women priests
The Daily Express

'We are pushing down a wall of the house'
The Daily Telegraph

WILL OF THE ALMIGHTY
The Daily Express

What is the well-dressed priestess wearing this year?
The Daily Express

Polite and prayerful flock takes the axe to an historic oak

Joy, dismay and warnings greet Synod vote for women
The Times

EVE ORDAINED
The Times

Synod accepts women priests
The Guardian

Are you going as a tart or a vicar?
The Guardian

Sikh women

In the Sikh tradition, there is a great emphasis on equality – between people of all races and backgrounds, and between men and women. All the ten Gurus were male but women and men can play the same and equal part in Sikh community life. Both may, if they are able to, read from the Guru Granth Sahib in the gurdwara.

A woman granthi, someone who can read the Guru Granth Sahib.

Sexuality – two Buddhist stories

These two traditional Buddhist stories are about men, women and sexuality – and about 'holding back' sometimes. They are also about compassion and openness.

When Every Other Love has left You

When he was a young man, the Buddha was very good looking. Some people were against him and his ideas, and played a trick on him to try to catch him out. They arranged for a well-known prostitute, whose clients were some of the most wealthy and influential men around, to pay him a visit.

The Buddha seemed to like her and they spent a long time together, talking about all kinds of things. By the end of the evening, she offered herself to him – but the Buddha only smiled and said, 'I will love you when no one else loves you. I will love you when every other love has left you.' She had never felt so hurt and insulted and she stormed out in a rage, swearing she would never speak to him again.

About forty years later, the Buddha was dying and was being carried on a stretcher, when he saw someone he recognised crouching in the shadows against a wall. She was dressed in rags and hunched over. The Buddha got down from his stretcher, crossed over to her and bent down. She was thin and gaunt, her face half-eaten with disease. Then, looking into her eyes, without speaking, the Buddha folded her gently in his arms. ■

Guru Nanak, the founder of Sikhism, spoke against the negative attitudes to women in India, at the time he lived:

> *It is through woman, the despised one, that we are conceived and from her that we are born. It is to woman that we get engaged and then married. She is our life-long friend and the survival of our race depends on her. On her death a man seeks another wife. Through woman we establish our social ties. Why denounce her, the one from whom even kings are born?*
>
> Guru Granth Sahib 473

Teenage Sikh girls playing music for worship at a gurdwara – with a traditional Eastern harmonium and a modern Western guitar.

The Woman, the Monks and the River

Once, as two Buddhist monks were on a journey, they came to a river bank where they saw a beautiful woman who, like them, needed to cross to the other side. The water was very deep so one of the monks picked her up and waded across the river, carrying her on his back. When they reached the river bank, he put her down and the two monks went on their way together.

They carried on walking, for miles and miles, until finally the other monk broke the silence. 'Have you forgotten you're a monk? What could you possibly have been thinking of – touching a woman, holding her body against yours?'

'I put the woman down at the edge of the river hours ago,' was his companion's reply, 'but you're still carrying her!' ■

The One and the Many: male and female images of God

There seem to be stories of thousands of gods and goddesses in the Hindu tradition yet most Hindus believe that God is One. A story in the Upanishads helps to show how both ideas can be true.

Salty, Sir

Although Svetaketu had learned many of the scriptures, his father thought he didn't really understand the nature of Brahman (God). So he said to him, 'Here, take this salt, put it in a glass of water and bring it back to me tomorrow.'

The next day, when his father asked for the salt, Svetaketu couldn't find it – it had all dissolved. 'Sip the water,' his father said. 'What does it taste like?' – 'Salty, Sir,' Svetaketu replied. 'Pour some out,' his father told him, 'try it again, and tell me what it tastes like now.' – 'Salty, Sir'.

'Right, now tip more away and drink from the bottom. What does *that* taste like?' – 'Salty, Sir' said Svetaketu.

'Salt in water,' his father explained, 'is like the pure Being that is in everything. You may not be able to sense it – and you certainly can't take it out – but it's *there*. That Being is the essence of everything, the "self" of all that exists, the Supreme Reality. You are that, Svetaketu.' ■

Hindus call the Supreme Reality, or Ultimate Spirit, **Brahman**. The whole of Creation is Brahman and Brahman is 'hidden' in everything. Some say that Brahman's images are like a pure light directed on to a prism. When the light hits it, it is refracted (broken up) into rainbow colours – but the original light is still there and still the same. Everything shows something of Brahman – every person, every animal, every plant, even rivers and stones. The nature of Brahman is especially clear in the many images that appear as gods or goddesses, and in the stories about them that people can understand. In one way, Brahman is both male and female; in another way, Brahman is neither male nor female. As the sun rises and the day becomes light, many Hindus say a prayer, called the **Gayatri Mantra**, which expresses the idea of Brahman as pure and infinite light.

Aum. Let us meditate on the radiance of the divine. May it inspire and light up our minds. Aum.

Some Hindus (Vaishnavas) take Vishnu as their supreme deity. They believe that, whenever there is trouble in the world, Vishnu comes down to earth with a human or animal identity: he destroys badness and puts goodness in its place. Vishnu is often shown sitting on a coiled snake, with the snake's seven heads shielding his head, like a canopy. Vishnu has a 'U'-shaped marking on his forehead and Vaishnavas often have this, too, as a sign of their devotion.

Vishnu has four arms and in them he holds a lotus flower, a conch, a disc and a club. His partner, Lakshmi, represents wealth and good fortune. She is shown as a beautiful golden woman, standing or sitting on a lotus – either alongside Vishnu or travelling with him. Lakshmi holds a lotus and coins.

The Song of Songs

In the Jewish tradition, God is seen in human relationships more than anywhere else: sometimes through a relationship between a parent and child, sometimes between a leader and the people… and very often between a man and a woman. The Bible is full of stories of couples and families and is very open about sexual relationships. From ancient times, Jews have seen sexual love as a gift from God and a celebration of life. One part of the Bible, in particular, expresses this idea. It is a book called the **Song of Songs** which is in the form of a love poem between a woman and a man. They are not named, but some say they were the Jewish King, Solomon, and the Ethiopian Queen of Sheba. Traditionally, Jews have interpreted the poem as an expression of the love between God and people – warm, passionate and devoted – and the union between a man and a woman as an image of the union of a soul that seeks God.

An image from an illustrated copy of the Song of Songs, made in Jerusalem, 1923.

My beloved is to me a bag of myrrh lodged between my breasts.
My beloved is to me a spray of henna blooms from the vineyards of E Gedi.
Oh you are fair, my darling, Oh you are fair, with your dove-like eyes.
And you, my beloved, are handsome, beautiful indeed!
Our couch is in a bower, cedars are the beams of our house; cypresses the rafters.

Song of Songs 1:13–17 (Jewish Publication Society)

Questions and activities

1 Since you were a child, what changes have you seen in the roles of men and women, and the relationship between them? It can be amongst people you know, people you hear about or maybe just a general feeling that you have. Do you think these changes are for the best?

2 Look at and talk about all the images of men and women (in photographs, drawings and words) in this chapter. What do they say about men and women in religious traditions and in society generally?

3 A On pages 64–65, read carefully and talk about the reasons for and against the ordination of women in the Christian Church. Which of the arguments from opposite sides can be paired with each other? Which points do you find most convincing? Can you think of any others – for or against?

   B On page 66, read what individual Christians said about the ordination of women. Which ones were *for* it and which ones *against*?

   C Look at the selection of newspaper headlines on pages 66–67. Which ones seem to be *for* the ordination of women, which ones *against* and which ones *neutral*? How can you tell?

   D Create a leaflet or poster to persuade other people to be **either** for **or** against the ordination of women. You can illustrate it with cartoons and words that people actually spoke.

4 A Read the story 'When Every Other Love Leaves You' on page 68. What did you expect to happen when the prostitute came to see the Buddha? Were you surprised at what he said? Who was the woman the Buddha saw from his stretcher? What did you think he was going to do? What does this story tell us about sexuality? Is sex the same as love?

   B In the story 'The Woman, the Monks and the River' on page 69, what did the monk mean by '…you're still carrying her'?

7 Food for Thought

Food talk

Have you ever known someone called 'out to lunch'? What does that mean? Has someone ever said to you, 'Don't make a meal of it!'? What were you doing? Or have you ever heard someone's ideas and plans described as 'half baked'? What was being described? There are lots of expressions in everyday speech that refer to food in some way. Why do you think that food imagery is used to describe personality, behaviour or even life itself? And why is food so important at times of celebration, like birthday parties, family outings and festivals? What we eat often matters as well as how much we eat. Why do you think this is?

Food is a vital part of everyone's life. We all have to eat and breathe to stay alive and they are the first things we did when we were born. But there is a difference, isn't there, between eating to live and living to eat. Do you know, or have you heard of, anyone who seems to 'live to eat'? What is life like for them?

When was the last time you said, 'I'm starving!'? Have you ever actually starved? Why do you think we use expressions like 'famished' or 'I could eat a horse!'? Look at the pictures on these pages. What attitudes to food and what kind of 'eating behaviour' do they show?

A mother feeding her child in a refugee camp, Sudan.

The Five, the Feast and the Fairy Godmother

He was homeless. He begged for food and money to buy it, but most people ignored him. One day a fairy godmother appeared to him and said, 'What's the matter?'

'I'm tired and hungry and cold – and fed up with begging,' he answered.

'I can help you,' she said gently. 'Find five other people, bring them to the warehouse over there and I will provide a feast for you all – absolutely free! You can stuff yourselves to your hearts' content. There'll be juicy roast meat, two kinds of potatoes, lots of vegetables and the finest wine – followed by ten of the richest puddings you can imagine. Then coffee, mints and liqueurs.'

With those mouth-watering words, the fairy godmother disappeared. Amazed and excited, he set out to invite five others to join him, thinking it would take no time at all to find five willing volunteers. The first person he met was a woman waiting for a bus.

'Excuse me,' he ventured, 'if you come with me, we can have the meal of our lives. There'll be roast meat with all the trimmings and as many sweets as you can think of. All we have to do is find four other people to take with us.'

She looked at him disdainfully. 'Thanks – but no thanks!' she said. 'I'm on a diet!' Then her bus drew up and she got on.

The next person he saw was a well-dressed young man and he stopped him and explained the fairy godmother's offer, adding that they would only need four other people to join them. The young man was horrified at the idea.

'That's outrageous – eating that amount of food when half the world is starving. We only need the most basic food for our needs. How could you just sit there and gorge all that, knowing that millions of children are dying of malnutrition?' And with that the young man stomped off.

He was puzzled by the first two reactions and beginning to wonder whether he'd ever get someone

to take up the offer, when he noticed a teenage girl who didn't look too well fed, either.

'I'm sorry,' she said, when he explained the offer, 'but I'm a vegetarian. It's appalling the way animals are treated and how they're killed for meat. They're cooped up for most of their lives and then brutalised – absolute agony. No thank you!' This time *he* moved on before he heard the really gruesome details.

Turning the corner, he bumped into a man of about fifty years of age who was jogging.

'Oh, I wouldn't touch the stuff!' the man said when he heard the plan. 'All that animal fat and refined carbohydrate! I want to know what I'm eating and where it's come from. We always do our own cooking. Everything's from packets and tins these days! I only eat organic wholefoods. Low fat, low salt and low sugar … high fibre … lots of raw, fresh fruit and vegetables.' And he carried on jogging.

He was on the point of giving up when he saw a priest coming down the street. That seemed like a real possibility at last. 'Any other time I'd be pleased to join you,' the priest explained, 'but today I'm on a sponsored fast to raise money for charity. I do hope you find your five.'

Utterly dejected, he trudged back and met another homeless person. When he told her everything that had happened, she was flabbergasted. 'You stupid fool!' she exclaimed. 'What's wrong with *us*? We're *all* starving!' She was right, of course, but how could he choose just four others?

Nervously, he entered the warehouse. There, waiting for him, was the fairy godmother and he told her his problem. 'Can you possibly take us all?' he asked. She smiled sweetly and stretched out her wand. And fifty of them sat down together to the meal of their lives. ■

Based on an original idea by Sue Kember at Feltham Community School

Food: celebration and identity

A Halal butcher's in Wembley, London.

A Jewish mother and son examining packets and tins to ensure that the ingredients are kosher.

Handmade sweets on sale for Hindu weddings, festivals and other special occasions.

Christmas dinner served with love in the crypt of St Botolph's Church, Aldgate, which gives homeless people food, advice and friendship all year round.

For many people, *what* they eat matters as much as *that* they eat. Food is an expression of our personality and our identity – who we are and who we belong with. This is especially true of people who find themselves in the minority in any situation. So in areas where people or their ancestors have settled from other places, there may be many food shops and restaurants selling and serving food 'from home'.

'Crisis at Christmas'

For the many millions of homeless people around the world, food often matters more than clothing or shelter. When people live on the streets or in poor, temporary accommodation where cooking is difficult, what they usually miss most is a cooked meal, served with love and eaten with dignity. In the West, they feel this most painfully at Christmas time. 'Crisis at Christmas' has been going for many years and is a special project to provide a 'taste of Christmas' for homeless people in British cities. It means that, if only for a few days in the year, there is a warm atmosphere, with tasty traditional food, lots of good company and festive fun.

Food and ritual

Have you ever heard someone saying something like 'You eat like a pig!'? Why do you think they use expressions like that and what are they really saying? One of the things that makes us different from other animals is the way we eat. We sometimes use 'tools' for eating, and we cook and flavour some of our food – which animals don't. Our 'rituals' for food are different from animals', too – and, in some ways, different from each other's. What food rituals do you have at home? How are they different from food rituals, say, at school, at a party or when eating on the street? What do these food rituals show about people's attitudes to food and about their attitudes to the people they're eating with?

Food rituals in many religious traditions show not only what people think about food but also what they feel about life or what they hope for, especially when food is part of a celebration. Quite often the taste, texture, shape and colour of food symbolise what the people believe or value. Some people recite prayers or blessings for food, before or after they eat, to show how grateful they are. Before they eat any of the food themselves, devout Hindus offer some to God, by placing it before a murti (image) in their kitchen: this means that they have to cook the food without tasting it.

A Buddhist woman offering food to a Buddhist monk in Thailand.

Symbolic foods for Easter in an Orthodox Christian home.

Food and discipline

What people *don't* eat often counts as much as what they do eat. Many religious traditions have food laws which say what people in that tradition should not eat. Some food laws apply all the time and are usually to do with eating food that involves killing animals. Jews and Muslims, for example, may eat certain kinds of meat but the animal must be killed in a way that causes the least pain.

Ahimsa

A Hindu ascetic.

Devout Hindus never eat meat. The principle behind this is **ahimsa** ('harmlessness'). It not only means not killing living beings directly but also not eating the flesh of a living being which has been killed. Many Hindus have fast days when they eat nothing or just drink water and have a little fruit. They find this is good for their body and soul. Some Hindus (ascetics) spend several years eating very little, as part of a whole disciplined, spiritual way of life in which they strive to have control over their bodies and become 'detached' from everyday life.

Some food laws and customs are only for certain occasions or certain times of the year. For example, some traditional Roman Catholics do not eat meat on Fridays, in remembrance of Good Friday, when Jesus died.

Lent

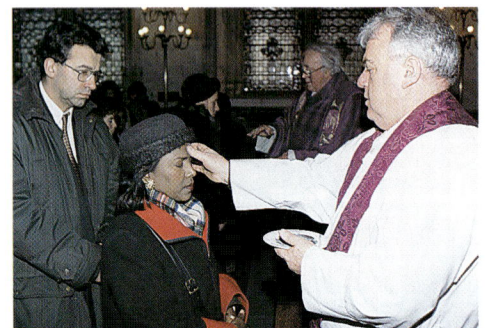

A Christian woman receiving ashes on her forehead on Ash Wednesday.

Lent is the six-week period leading up to Easter: Christians remember the forty days when Jesus fasted and prayed in the wilderness. Many Christians 'fast' in Lent which is an important time for prayer, self-reflection, confession and Bible study. Some give up their favourite foods or do not eat meat then. Orthodox Christian communities often have 'steps' in fasting which get more disciplined as Lent progresses: it may start with not eating meat or drinking wine, then cutting out fish, then dairy foods, then sweet things… until there is a total fast on Good Friday. Lent begins with 'Ash Wednesday' when Christians receive ashes on their foreheads as a symbol of repentance and fasting.

Ital

If you are going to reach into life everliving, you must eat divinely, of life everliving. It's that simple.

Tracy Nicholas, *Rastafari: A Way of Life*, Anchor Books, 1979

Ital food for sale in Ladbroke Grove.

Ital foods are 'total' foods: they are not contaminated or 'de-natured' by processing that adds or takes anything away from the food's own goodness. Rastas see the human body as one of the miracles of nature, a reflection of Jah (God) which should be treated as such. They believe that anything a man or woman does becomes part of what he or she is. When Jah created the first people, he said that all herbs bearing seeds and all trees bearing fruit would be food for them. So devout Rastas refuse to spoil and desecrate their bodies by eating dead flesh: only life can give life. They say that we should not make our bodies into a 'cemetery' and they see tinned and packaged foods as dead and 'buried'. In Jamaica, Rastas drink and cook with rain water because tap water has many unnatural additives. They eat what comes from the soil and call this food **agridishes**. They say that the ital diet is the key to their good health and long life.

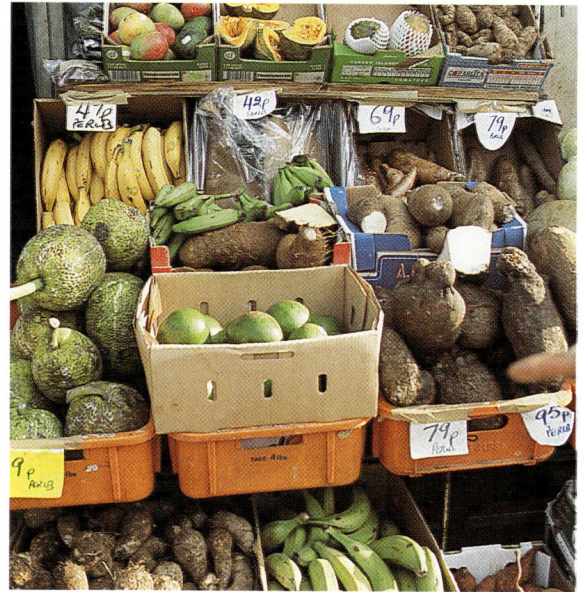

There is today a greater menace to civilisation than that of war. The name of this menace is malnutrition. We eat too much, and most of what we eat is poison to our system. Half of what we eat keeps us alive; the other half keeps the physician alive.

A popular dish in Jamaica is rice and peas (beans), often flavoured with meat. For the ital version, Rastas grate coconut to produce a delicious milk and use it to cook the rice, adding many different vegetables for taste and nutrition. Rastas have a way of peeling oranges without losing any of the fruit and juice.

Some Rastas do not use metal, glass or china dishes and utensils: they eat from coconut bowls with their fingers or with utensils made from coconut shells or wood. Most say this is because of their cultural roots in Africa. Men and women share in the preparation of ital food.

Siyyam– fasting in the Islamic tradition

Siyyam, fasting, is an important part of the Islamic tradition. Every year in the month of Ramadan, all adult Muslims have to fast during the hours of daylight – unless there are health reasons why they cannot.

Ramadan is a special month because it was during this month that the Prophet Muhammad received the Qur'an.

A Muslim family breaking fast during Ramadan.

Fasting for a limited period is not bad for the health and can be good for the body. Going without food and water for a long time helps people feel what it's like to be starving and it helps them to feel compassion for people who are starving and suffering. These are not the main reasons for the Ramadan fast, however. It is really a personal discipline, a way of controlling the body and knowing that there is more to life than satisfying the appetite.

Sadi Shiraz, a Muslim storyteller, tells this story:

Dead or Alive

Once two friends were travelling together. One of them hardly ever ate anything and was quite thin, but the other always ate too much and was quite fat. Sadly, they were both suspected of spying and were put in prison – in separate cells. The conditions in the jail were terrible and there was very little food.

After a week, when it was realised they were innocent after all, the order came for them to be released and the guards opened their cell doors to let them go free. The thin man was fine but the fat man was dead. Everyone was shocked and puzzled. 'You'd think it would be the other way round, if anything!' the guards said in amazement. 'You'd think the fat man, with his fat to live off, would have a chance of staying alive but the thin man would just waste away with hunger. It just doesn't make sense!'

Abdul Ahmed and his family own a restaurant that is open every day of the year, at midday and in the evening. He works there himself, supervising the cooking and service to the customers. All his staff are Muslims. When he was asked what it is like to keep the Ramadan fast, surrounded by delicious smells and people tucking into tasty food, he smiled and said:

You can get used to anything if you really want to! And we do want to! You just ignore it, really. You just try to switch off any hunger you're feeling. It's like it's there but it's not affecting you in the normal way. But it's harder for the chef than for me because he has to cook without tasting and so he sometimes makes mistakes! When that happens, we joke with our regular customers that it's a special Ramadan recipe!

When they're fasting, people often feel a bit weak and tired during the afternoon. That's the hardest time of the day during Ramadan, too, but our restaurant is closed then so we can all rest or have a nap. But even if it's hard, it's still very good. Fasting is something that we give but it is also something that we receive – a very special feeling of being close to everything in Islam, close to the life of The Prophet, peace be upon him, and close to the revelation from Allah. Nothing we could ever do would be too much for that.

'Oh, yes, it does!' said a wise one among them. 'It would have been much more surprising, the other way round. You see, the fat one was used to eating a lot and so he couldn't resist hunger: that's why he died. But the thin one was used to not eating very much so he could resist hunger: that's why he survived.' ■

Sadi Shiraz said that this means that if you are sensible and practise moderation, you can face calamities with courage. If you're an extremist, however, when you are forced to practise moderation, you find it hard – and you die.

Adapted from Ashraf Abu Turab and Zia Sardar (eds.),
A Time to Speak: Anecdotes from Sadi Shiraz, The Islamic Foundation, 1980

Three weeks, three days and three minutes

Rabbi Hugo Gryn grew up in eastern Europe and, when he was a teenager, his whole community was rounded up by the Nazis and taken to a concentration camp. Conditions were hard and food was in very short supply. Afterwards, he often remembered the festival of **Hanukkah** (the Jewish winter festival of light) in the camp. He remembered how they had had to improvise and something he learned there and then about food.

I did not learn the lesson about faith in a theological college – that came much later, but in a miserable little concentration camp… It was the cold winter of 1944 and, although we had nothing like calendars, my father who was my fellow prisoner there took me and some of our friends to a corner in our barrack. He announced that it was the eve of Hanukkah, produced a curious-shaped clay bowl and began to light a wick immersed in his precious, but now melted, margarine ration. Before he could recite the blessing, I protested at this waste of food. He looked at me – then at the lamp – and finally said: 'You and I have seen that it is possible to live up to three weeks without food. We once lived almost three days without water. But you cannot live properly for three minutes without hope.'

Rabbi Hugo Gryn, about 40 years later, lighting candles at a children's Hanukkah party.

Questions and activities

1   Make two columns. In the left hand column, list everyday expressions related to *food*, *meals* and *eating* that are an image of life or human personality – like 'out to lunch', 'making a meal of it'. In the right hand column, write what each expression means. Compare your list with a partner and see what conclusions you can draw. Why do you think food imagery is used so much?

2   Read the story 'The Five, the Feast and the Fairy Godmother' on pages 76–77.
    A   Copy and complete the following chart to show the different attitudes to food that people in the story have.

Character in the story	Reason for not going to the feast
woman waiting for bus	on a diet
	wrong to eat a lot when there's so much starvation
teenage girl	
	on a sponsored fast for charity

    B   Why do you think the fairy godmother, in the beginning, made the young homeless man find five other people to join him – why didn't she just give him the meal by himself?
    C   Why do you think the fairy godmother, in the end, provided the meal for about fifty people?
    D   What effect do you think the five people who refused the feast, had on the young homeless man's ideas about food?
    E   Would the feast make life easier or harder for the young homeless people afterwards?
    F   If you'd been asked to go to the feast, how would you have responded – and why?

3   What are the similarities and differences between fasting, starving and dieting? You could present this as a chart.

4   Read about 'Crisis at Christmas' on page 78. Some homeless people, who have Christmas meals in one of the centres, say it makes it very hard for them to go back to their 'normal' life afterwards. If you were in their position, do you think you would find that?

5   Design a balanced meal that is in keeping with the ital diet, choosing ingredients which are available where you live. What difficulties would Rastas have in keeping to an ital diet in Britain?

6   Read carefully the story 'Dead or Alive' on pages 82–83. What do you think Sadi Shiraz means by 'practise moderation'? Do you agree with his point – why? What else could this apply to, apart from eating?

8 And then what?

This chapter is about:

- the fact of death and the questions it raises
- the attitudes of different religions to death, and their beliefs about death and beyond
- the Islamic view of death and the after-life
- a Christian funeral director's perspective on death
- death and rebirth in the Hindu tradition
- death and rebirth in the Sikh tradition

What is 'dead'?

It is natural for us to be interested in the idea of death and want to understand what it means. It may be a frightening idea or a reason to be really sad. Being faced with the idea of a final moment of living might make us wonder what life is for and what it means. What does 'dead' mean to you?

This poem deals bluntly with the fact that physical death comes to us all eventually. It is the great equaliser and no one can avoid it.

Death Lib

*The liberating thing about death
is in its fairness to women,
its acceptance of blacks,
its special consideration for the sick.*

*And I like the way
that children aren't excluded,
homosexuals are welcomed,
and militants aren't banned.*

*The really wonderful thing about death
is that all major religions agree on it,
all beliefs take you there,
all philosophy bows before it,
all arguments end there.*

*Con men can't con it
Thieves can't nick it
Bullies can't scare it
Magicians can't trick it.*

*Boxers can't punch it
Nor critics dismiss it
Don't knows can't not know
The lazy can't miss it.*

*Governments can't ban it
Or the army defuse it
Judges can't jail it
Lawyers can't sue it.*

*Capitalists can't bribe it
Socialists can't share it
Terrorists can't jump it
The Third World aren't spared it.*

*Scientists can't quell it
Nor can they disprove it
Doctors can't cure it
Surgeons can't move it.*

*Einstein can't halve it
Guevara can't free it
The thing about dead
Is we're all gonna be it.*

Steve Turner, in *Nice and Nasty*, Razor Books &
Marshall Morgan & Scott, 1980

A Tibetan Buddhist saying goes:

Since our lives are short and it is certain that we will die,
When suddenly we are assailed by the savage conditions of death,
Like a flame in a strong wind
Flickering and unstable at every moment,
Engage now in the search for the meaning that life holds.

Translated by John Peacock

Is death the end?

Although we all experience loss and grief, no one reacts to death in the same way. Our feelings are intensely personal, and may be coloured by our cultural or religious background. We may ask ourselves: Is death really the end? Is there 'life' after death? These belong to the 'big questions about life' – the questions that we may not all have a fixed answer to. We cannot absolutely answer the question 'What is dead?' although the law in many countries assumes that we know what dying, death and life are, and can tell when one stops and the other begins. On the other hand, other cultures have a different definition of death. For instance, among a group in Papua New Guinea, someone who is only unconscious is described as 'dead' and so someone might 'die' many times.

The end or the beginning?

Birth and death are two life events – the only two – which happen to everyone, and all religions are concerned with them. Both birth and death are marked by ceremonies which guide the person from one stage of existence to another. Most religions say that a person lives on after death in some way. Some religions believe in a physical resurrection, some in living on in people's hearts and others believe in reincarnation and eventually, liberation.

The Day of the Dead

Each October in Mexico there is a three-day festival known as 'The Day of the Dead' when families prepare to welcome the spirits of the dead. It is a time for remembering loved ones who have died but whose memory is cherished and celebrated. People buy traditional 'pan de muertos' (the 'bread of the dead') from the bakers, sugar skulls from the confectioners, and bunches of colourful marigolds – the flowers of the dead – from the market.

A 'dressed skeleton' in a poster for an exhibition of 'Day of the Dead' art.

The Islamic view: the Garden of Paradise

When a person dies, the angels say: 'What has he sent in advance?' But humans say: 'What has he left behind?'

Saying of the Prophet Muhammad

Islam teaches that, when someone dies, their soul is taken into the charge of the angel of death, and on the Day of Judgement everyone will be raised up from the dead to account for their beliefs and actions. People whose good deeds outweigh the bad will go to **Al-Jannah** (Paradise). People whose bad deeds are heavier will be thrown into the Fire of Hell, and given hot water to drink and bitter fruit to eat.

The Qur'an has many images of heaven and hell. In Al-Jannah everyone will be in the prime of youth. It is a lovely, green, enclosed garden, with flowering plants and trees, and hidden from view. It has four sweetly scented streams, flowing from a fountain. There is no hatred or bad feeling: 'Where they shall hear no word of vanity; and where there is a bubbling spring'(Surah 88: 11f).

Although we cannot really imagine Paradise, as it belongs to another stage of existence, it is a vivid and powerful image.

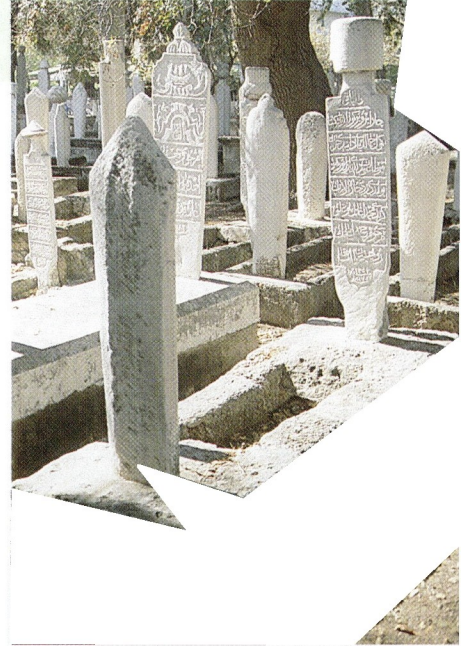

Muslim gravestones, in a traditional form, with 'symbolic' handles.

Reclining in the garden on raised thrones,
They will see there neither
The sun's excessive heat,
Nor the moon's excessive cold.

And the shades of the Garden
Will come low over them
And the bunches of fruit
There will hang low in humility.

And amongst them will be
Passed round vessels of silver
And goblets of crystal.

Surah 86: 13-15

Prayer carpets are often designed with floral patterns. They remind Muslims that God is the Creator of all things, and they direct their thoughts to Paradise.

An interview with a Christian funeral director

Audrey Gamlin is a practising Christian and a funeral director in London. She talks about her experience of dealing with death and bereavement. She describes a 'typical' Christian funeral – both burial and cremation; and gives some insight into the impact of her Christian beliefs on her work.

Being a funeral director is very complicated. We have to know the laws about death and funerals, and all the requirements and rituals of different religions. If the family is very upset or angry, I listen – and comfort them as much as I can. If they need guidance, I suggest someone they can talk to, such as a minister.

I believe God has sent me to do this job and it's my faith that keeps me going, in dealing with death every day. But it's not for me to say what I believe about death so I don't talk about heaven or where the dead person has gone. I'm not afraid of what happens after death. I believe I'm going to a better world where I'll see my friends and family again. Many people are afraid of their own death and their tears are often as much for themselves as for the dead person. I see a difference between people who have a particular belief and people who don't. You can never be fully prepared for death but you need to talk about it and tell children about it.

About 80 per cent of funerals are cremations – partly because churches are running out of space for graves or relatives don't want to look after the grave. About 70 per cent of our customers have no deep belief but they'd probably say they were Church of England. Anyone who says they are can have a Christian funeral service. If it's a Christian funeral, we ask their minister to officiate in the church and at the cemetery or crematorium. If the person didn't belong to a particular church, we make sure a minister and church are available. We collect the body, embalm it and put in the coffin. On the day of the funeral, we take the coffin in a hearse to the house, where we collect the mourners and make our way slowly to the church.

Sometimes, if the deceased was a Roman Catholic, the coffin lies overnight in front of the altar at church and a Requiem Mass is said in the morning. Some Irish Catholics take the coffin home before the funeral so that family and friends can gather to take a last look at the body, to show their respect, to say prayers for the dead person and to celebrate their life. It's called a 'wake' because people are keeping watch over the corpse. Some people say you need to see the body to face the fact that they are dead.

The service is full of hope and comfort, with words from John's Gospel: 'I am the resurrection and the life, says the Lord: whoever believes in me, even though they die, yet shall they live, and whoever lives and believes in me shall never die.'

If it's a burial, the coffin is taken to the cemetery after the service and placed on web ropes by the side of the grave. It's lowered into the grave, and the minister commits the body to the earth.

In a cremation, the coffin is placed on a bench with rollers. Prayers are said and the coffin is rolled away behind curtains, into the furnace. The body takes about 30 to 45 minutes to burn. The heat is so intense that the coffin vaporises. The 'brass' handles are now made of plastic so that they'll melt too. The remains are collected in a tray and, when cool, ground to a fine powder. The name plate from the coffin goes on the tray so we know whose ashes they are. We collect the ashes in an urn the next day and the family gets them from us. Many Christians scatter the ashes in the local churchyard and plant a flower in memory of the deceased.

A coffin being lined at a funeral director's.

Water and fire: death and rebirth in the Hindu tradition

Many Hindus come to die and be cremated at Varanasi in India. Some say that it will release their soul to continue its journey. The body is immersed in the River Ganges and water splashed into the uncovered mouth. When the pyre is cold, the ashes are gathered and scattered on the Ganges with marigold petals. Prayers and hymns are recited from the Hindu scriptures, such as this from the Bhagavad Gita:

Burning ghats at Varanasi, India.

> *For the death of those born is certain, and the birth of the dead is certain; therefore do not grieve about what is inevitable.*

And this:

> *May your eyesight return to the sun, your life's breath to the winds; may your water mingle with the ocean and your matter become one with the earth. The indestructible spirit passes on into another body according to the actions performed in this life.*
>
> Rig Veda

Babies are not burned but their bodies are weighted with stones, rowed to the middle of the river and dropped into 'Mother Ganges' waiting arms. Later, a tiny lamp may be floated downstream, symbolising the departing spirit.

Hindus believe that we are in a cycle of many births, deaths and rebirths (samskaras). Death is not the end of life but another stage. Cremation is the sixteenth samskara, or final stage, in a Hindu's physical life. Hindu scriptures teach that when the skull cracks in the fire, the **atman** (soul) escapes into the atmosphere. It will either be reborn or achieve spiritual freedom, and become one with Brahman – that which is real and undying.

> *As a person casts off worn-out clothes and puts on other new ones, so does the soul cast off worn-out bodies and enters other new ones.*
>
> Bhagavad Gita 2: 22

The various stages of life are like a circle and so the elements used in birth rituals are also used in death rituals. The fire lit on the twelfth day after birth, when the baby's name is chosen, is also the fire which consumes the body at death. Fire is a very powerful force in the Hindu tradition: it causes destruction in the world but it also warms every living thing. It represents the vital energy of the universe.

When Hindus greet each other with affection and respect, they crack their knuckles on their heads. Some say this is because of the custom of staying at a funeral pyre until the cracking of the bones can be heard. So cracking knuckles is a way of saying: I will love you until after you are dead.

For some Hindus (Shaivas), Shiva is the Supreme Lord who brings together opposites – Creation and destruction, good and evil, discipline and spontaneity, kindness and ferocity... He has three eyes to see the past, the present and the future. He is the Lord of time, carrying the moon in his matted hair. Sometimes he is shown carrying a noose or wearing a garland. As in this image, he is often shown as a cosmic dancer, stamping out evil and beating out the rhythm of the universe with his small drum shaped like an hour-glass.

A Sikh view of death

Relatives may recite the hymn of peace, the Sukhmani, of Guru Arjan to a dying person. They can take comfort in it as it ends with the words:

> *Why be too attached to home and family? They are short-lived like flowers in a garden. Think of God, who provides everything that you have. Leave everything else behind.*
>
> Adi Granth 50

For Sikhs, death is liberation from this impermanent, changing world. If someone lives in union with God, they are not afraid of death. Death is the moment when union with God is complete and the cares of human life disappear. These words, often spoken at a Sikh funeral service, emphasise that idea:

> *Good friends! Strange is God's creation.*
> *One dies; another still claims to live for ever.*
> *Who can explain this mystery?*
> *Humankind is gripped by lust, envy and worldly attachments*
> *And has put God out of mind.*
> *Why do you behave as though this body is permanent?*
> *It passes like the dream in the night.*
> *Whatever you see, it is sure to pass away*
> *Like the shadow of a moving cloud.*
> *Nanak! They who know this world is impermanent*
> *Seek protection in the name of the Lord.*
>
> Guru Teg Bahadur (Adi Granth 219)

The tradition among Sikhs is to cremate the body as soon after death as possible. The **ardas**, the central Sikh prayer, and other hymns, are recited several times as the body is prepared and the funeral fire is lit. The **sohilla** (the evening prayer) is also read because Sikhs think of death as sleep – with the believer waking up to a new state. The sohilla is not a mournful prayer but a hymn of praise to God.

Sikhs say that the best way of coming to terms with a death is to read the scriptures or to recite God's name. Sikhs do not put up gravestones or monuments to the dead but believe that their memory lives on through the good things they did in their lifetime.

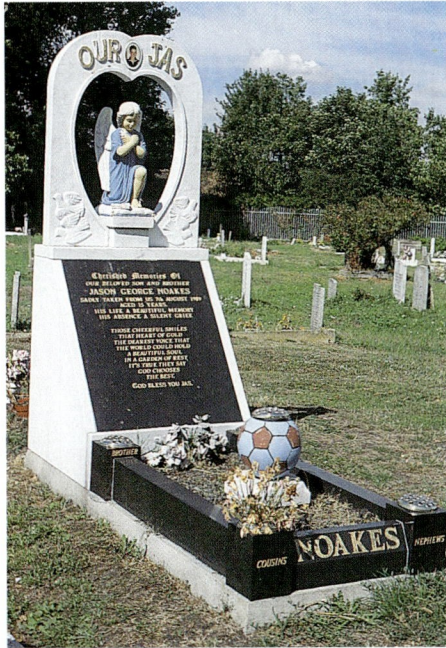

Gravestones in a
British public
cemetery showing a
range of beliefs and
attitudes to death.

Index